WRITING AND SELLING MAGAZINE ARTICLES

OMER HENRY

Writing and Selling

Magazine

Articles

BOSTON   The Writer, Inc.   PUBLISHERS

FOREWORD

If you are attempting to learn how to write magazine articles that will sell, you will, I hope, find in this book the precise aid you need. It outlines in specific detail the methods many successful writers use. Regardless of your background, academic training, or literary ability, you can learn to utilize and apply these methods. The process is simple and, furthermore, you do not need either magic wand or crystal ball as apparatus.

In the following pages, I shall describe and discuss hundreds of active markets—newspapers and small magazines of which you may never have heard. Publications in your own section of the country, your state, and perhaps even in your own city will be included as markets for articles of various kinds.

Writing and Selling Magazine Articles shows you what sort of articles editors want, why they want that kind of material, and step-by-step methods of preparing it.

"How long," you may ask, "must I serve as an apprentice? When may I become a selling writer?"

When you have learned to apply the principles explained and outlined in this book, editors will buy your manuscripts. Even more, editors will ask you to prepare articles for them. Once you thoroughly understand how to proceed, you have an "Open Sesame" to editorial checks.

Here is a blueprint, marking every step of the way to that kind of success. I hope that you use it well.

Omer Henry

CONTENTS

Chapter I

FUNDAMENTALS OF SUCCESSFUL ARTICLE WRITING

••

YOU WANT to sell magazine articles for money. This is your objective. In order to achieve that end you are willing to work conscientiously. But you are businesslike. You want to know that when you have performed your part of the contract, there will be a reward for you—dollars on the desk.

Consider today's non-fiction writers. Most of them were not appearing in magazines five or ten years ago, or even, in many cases, one year ago. New by-lines appear in almost every issue of a magazine. These new writers are ordinary men and women who have learned to put a magazine article together. If they can do this, so can you.

There is no mystery about the process of writing articles that will sell. But you must begin—not with dreams, wishes, and half-truths but with a firm foundation—if you are to succeed.

Here is that foundation.

WHAT IS A MAGAZINE ARTICLE?

A good place to start is with a definition. We may define a magazine article as a short prose composition designed to impart information interestingly.

1

If such an article is under 500 words in length, it may be called a filler. Longer articles are called features. It is seldom that a feature article runs more than 5,000 words in length, and 2,500 words is a far more popular length. Thousands of articles are much shorter than this.

The foregoing facts tell you that it would be difficult to write an acceptable magazine article on the subject of International Public Relations. In order to treat such a topic adequately, even a skilled writer would require far more space than a magazine article generally occupies. A magazine article must deal with a subject which can be presented effectively in, at most, a few thousand words. Thus you might write an article about "How Miami Cleaned Up the Automobile Insurance Claims Racket," not "The Automobile Insurance Claims Racket." Limiting your subject for a magazine article in this way enables you to treat your material comprehensively in the short space allotted to a magazine article.

Your Objective

Perhaps more would-be writers fail because they do not comprehend their function as writers than for any other one reason.

"I have a wonderful story," one of my students told me. "It is so filled with emotion that it makes me forget everything and everybody but that story. I cry each time I read it."

If this woman were writing the story for herself, it would undoubtedly be a spectacular success. But for a million magazine readers, it might be a dismal failure. Therefore, an editor considering an article for publication weighs its value not to the author but to his readers.

This, then, should make rather clear the article writer's objective. It is to produce a manuscript which will make a genuine appeal to the reader. In preparing an article, the professional writer thinks not of himself but of his readers. They demand his full attention. He attempts to put into his article information, drama, significance that will satisfy the group of readers for whom he is writing. This brings us to another important consideration: Your reader.

WHO IS YOUR READER?

If your prospective reader is a junior high school boy, you may reasonably expect him to take an interest in high school sports, soapbox derbies, and little league baseball. He knows something of these subjects and is keenly interested in them. If you can give him new information on one of these subjects, the editor of a publication for junior high school boys will very likely be interested in your offering.

This same material, however, would get a distinctly chilly reception in the offices of *Everywoman's Family Circle, Woman's Day,* or *Popular Mechanics.* The reason is simple: These subjects are light years removed from the specific interests of those who read the foregoing magazines.

Thus, it is necessary that you know your reader. Only when you understand him are you in a position to select subjects in which he will be interested. And the stronger his interest, other elements being equal, the more appropriate your subject matter. Only if you can identify your reader can you hope to produce articles that will truly appeal to him. By studying the magazine to which you hope to submit your article manuscript, you will come to understand the group of people whom the editor knows as his readers. When you can visualize these readers as the editor sees them, you will be able to produce articles the editor is likely to buy.

Analysis

"It seems to me," you say, "that one could spend a great amount of time studying magazines. Aren't there any short cuts?"

There are short cuts. I shall mention two of them:

1. Select the type of magazine for which you wish to write. Devote your time to this general field rather than to the entire range of magazines.

2. Learn to analyze published articles.

An analysis is a detailed consideration of the components of an article—a study to determine its ingredients and how they fit into the needs of a particular periodical. It includes a consideration of:

a. The purpose of the publication.

b. Who are the readers?

c. Why does this article appeal to these readers?

d. How is the article organized? Is it presented effectively? If so, by what devices?

e. Is the presentation attractive to the readers of this magazine? Does the title invite the reader to read further? Does the lead lure the reader on?

f. Is the article more and more interesting as it advances? How did the author keep the interest from lagging?

g. Is there a high interest point in the article? If so, what is it? Where is it in relation to the end of the article?

h. Does this article have definite direction, that is, does it set out to accomplish something and move in that direction?

i. What is the most significant part of the article? Where is it placed in relation to the article—at the beginning, middle, or end?

k. Is the article timely? Could it have been made timely? Would that have improved it?

l. What can you say of the end of the article? Does it leave the reader convinced? Satisfied? Pleased?

I suggest that you work with pencil and paper in making such an analysis. Write the answers to each of the foregoing points.

When you have analyzed a few articles in a given publication, you will have a rather definite understanding of what the editor wants to give his readers. This will certainly help you to meet this editor's requirements.

LITERARY AGENTS

Many beginning writers feel that if they had literary agents their rejection slips would turn into hundred-dollar checks overnight. "I'd let my agent tell me what to write and how to write it," one beginning writer told me, "and then I'd write it and he'd sell it."

This statement illustrates the widespread misunderstanding of literary agents and their work.

There are two distinct types of literary agents—one type advertises and the other does not. The former offers to assist the writer in making his material suitable for publication and, when that is done, to sell it. For this service he charges a reading fee plus, if the manuscript sells, a regular commission. Some of these agents offer to refund the reading fee if the material sells.

To the amateur writer who has been drawing only rejection slips for his work, this sounds like a dream come true. In his enthusiasm he sends off his manuscript with a reading fee and, in due time, he gets a letter of criticism. It is quite likely, too, that he gets a bale of advertising material designed to bring in more reading fees.

Occasionally such an agent sells a manuscript for a client. But this is so infrequent that it can be disregarded. Such an agent is actually a critic of sorts. His major income is from reading fees, not from the commissions on sales. This is potent evidence that he is most unlikely to sell your literary wares.

The other type of literary agent, the one who does not advertise, has an entirely different approach. He charges no reading fee but derives his entire compensation from commissions on sales he makes for writers.

Such an agent will accept a writer only if he feels it would be a good business proposition for him to do so. An agent of this caliber is a definite asset to a writer. But it is seldom that the amateur writer can produce manuscripts of high enough quality to get an agent of this type. The hard fact is that the literary agent has no magic formula by which he can sell a worthless manuscript. Moreover, if the offering is worth publishing, you probably can sell it yourself.

You should busy yourself in learning the profession of writing salable manuscripts. When you have acquired a considerable degree of skill as a writer, you can make good use of the non-advertising agent. Don't look upon the agent as a short cut to literary success. He is no such thing.

FINDING A NEW ANGLE

You have within your being an important ingredient of success. If you learn to utilize this element, you can speed your progress as a writer. What is this element? How should you use it?

The element is individuality—originality. This simply means that you, by your personal way of thinking, can transform old material into something new, fresh, and publishable. How?

Consider, for instance, the Washington Monument as subject matter for an article. All the world knows of this famous memorial in the nation's capital; hundreds of articles have been written about it. This would indicate that it is poor material for a magazine article. Yet, every February you find new stories in print about this Monument.

How do writers manage to sell such stories?

By finding new angles—individuality. For instance: Not long ago I decided to do a story about the Monument. I asked myself what new information I could give. What would my personal angle be? A bit of research gave me the answer. I would tell the truly fantastic facts of this national shrine. I did this in an article called "Fantastic Washington Monument." *Highway* magazine published it.

Another writer found a different angle: about the only thing that hasn't happened in the Washington Monument, he concluded after researching the subject, is that Washington never slept in it. He wrote the article, outlining some of the startling things that happened in the Washington Monument, and *This Week* published it.

Still another writer's research for a story about this Monument led him to the conclusion that the Monument has been kicked around. He wrote an article, called it "The Monument That Was Kicked Around," and sold it to *Cosmopolitan* magazine.

These are examples of making something new and readable out of an old subject. Writers do it every day by giving their work an original angle. You may utilize this technique on any kind of article. Just give it some thought. Ask yourself what new and intriguing information you can give about your subject. Then make a good case for your thesis. This new angle can help you over the hump to many a sale.

Another stone in the foundation of your success as a writer is your enthusiasm. The dictionary says that enthusiasm is strong excitement of feeling on behalf of a cause or a subject; ardent and imaginative zeal or interest; fervor. This characteristic can help you in your writing. It can transform a dull, insipid paragraph into exciting reading. For example:

> In the United States National Museum in Washington you may see a large and interesting collection of minerals and gemstones which have been gathered from all over the world. Some of these are in the rough as they came from the mine, others are cut and polished, and still others are in a semi-polished state.

That paragraph gives considerable information. It is understandable, but it hasn't one spark of life. It has nothing to lure the reader on, nothing to excite him, and little, in fact, to reward him for reading. It is so dull that an editor would never approve it. It could be intriguing. What it needs is life, enthusiasm. Let us see if we can inject into it this all-important element.

> Americans own fabulous treasures. Among them, housed in the United States National Museum, is the world's great-

est collection of precious stones. Rubies and pearls, opals and sapphires, diamonds and emeralds in vast profusion sparkle and gleam like the jewels in Aladdin's cave.

There, in approximately the same space as the first example, you have generated interest in the reader. You have your reader rushing on breathlessly to learn more of this exciting subject, and he is enthralled by the vista before him.

How did it happen? What caused this transformation?

It was the writer's enthusiasm. He saw something of compelling interest and put it before his readers in a fascinating manner. He appealed to the readers' imagination and showed his own strong excitement about these fabulous treasures. Put this element of enthusiasm into your articles. It will help you to make sale after sale.

FICTION TECHNIQUES FOR NON-FICTION

You will do well, at the very beginning of your career as a writer, to comprehend fully one terrifically important principle about writing, i.e., you must make your article intriguing.

It is not enough to pack an article with new and useful information. That is valueless unless someone reads it. And, in order to make your work readable, you must enliven it with every device at your command.

You will use a title that demands that the reader peruse your article. And, when you begin the first paragraph—the lead—you will make sure that you lure the reader on. You will deliberately work into these fifty to seventy-five words a "narrative hook" which will ensnare the reader, making him unwilling to put down the magazine until he has read the last satisfying word of your article.

Now that you have the article under way, you cannot let up on the interest or let the article drift—not if you hope to sell it. The intriguing quality of your piece must grow and grow and grow as the article progresses. You will utilize dialogue. You will play one force against another. You will indulge in suspense, even as the skilled fiction writer.

"In many respects," says the outstandingly successful author Maurice Zolotow, "the successful article should be a work of art, like the short story—a created whole, with a beginning, a middle, and an end, with climaxes, buildups, tensions, drama expressed in dialogue, and even sentiment and feeling."

Perhaps an illustration or two would be helpful:

The White House

The White House is the home of our President. It is a beautiful mansion standing among stately trees in the 1600 block of Pennsylvania Avenue in Washington. Thousands of people visit it each month. They walk through the history-packed rooms where other thousands of fellow Americans have preceded them.

This is literate writing. It tells something of the White House. But it is wholly unsuitable for publication in a magazine story because it lacks interest. Contrast it with the following:

HEART OF THE NATION

In the nation's capital stands United States' most famous home. Even though practically every school child recognizes it, few adults—including our most astute statesmen—comprehend its full significance.

Its history is packed with thousands of events ranging from pathetic to joyful, superstitious to the superlatively wise, inconsequential to world-moving.

This 132-room mansion set on an 18-acre plot of land covered with beautiful flowers, majestic trees, ancient boxwood, and sparkling fountains is the White House, the home of our Presidents.

Look at these two titles: "The White House" and "Heart of the Nation." Which of these arouses in you a desire to read further? Which is the more inviting?

Certainly it is the second. The first tells you flatly that the article is about the White House. But that fails to intrigue you; it offers nothing to whet your interest. You already know about the White House. This title, therefore, offers you nothing. You pass it up—and so would other readers.

But the other—"Heart of the Nation"—is different. It arouses your curiosity. What is the Heart of the Nation? You would like to know, and so you read on to learn the answer. In the second example you find paragraph one intensifies the curiosity which the title arouses in you. What, you wonder, is the nation's most famous home? What is its significance—such significance that even our most astute statesmen do not fully comprehend it? This is designed to intrigue the reader, to cause him to read on.

Paragraph two carries out the same plan. Here you find a promise of amusement, of pathos, joy, wisdom. This is inviting. And you, being human, want to read more of this article which promises to amuse you and even give you useful information.

Thus, in the second example, the writer used an approach more like that of a fiction writer. By doing so he produced copy far more acceptable than that in the first example. This is a technique of the modern article.

We may state the foregoing fact thus: The modern magazine article and the fiction story are sisters under the skin. Therefore, you may advantageously utilize fiction technique in your articles. This will help to make sale after sale.

CAN YOU SELL YOUR ARTICLES?

Though the market for articles today is far greater than ever before and the financial rewards high, you may wonder what your chances of success are. Will editors buy articles from an unknown? What can you expect to make as an income from your writing?

Let us look at these questions one at a time.

Can you, an unknown writer, sell your article manuscripts?

You most certainly can! Pick up any issue of a writer's magazine, and you will find many statements like this from editors of various magazines using non-fiction: "We are in the process of trying to build up a list of free-lance writers upon whom we can call for material from time to time . . ."

"Currently we are seeking good articles on the following subjects . . ."

"We are looking for timely articles—controversy, social problems, outstanding personalities, entertainment, sports, travel, science, adventure . . ."

"We use articles on restaurants and entertainment, travel, etc. and pay from $250 to $750 for them. Buy pix submitted with articles at $150 to $300."

Read the editors' complete specifications. You will not find one word about the authors. Editors are interested not in who does the article, but in the piece itself. If you, an unknown, produce an article that appeals to the editor, he will buy it. This is happening hundreds of times every day.

What can you expect in the way of income?

That depends upon your ability, the type of market you seek, and the time you put into the business. I have on my desk a letter from the editor of a trade publication. He wants three interviews, each approximately 1,500 words long. And the price? Two hundred dollars per article for text alone!

Thousands of men and women earn $500 to $5,000 a year from writing as an avocation. If you learn the profession and become a full-time writer, you may earn many times that amount in the run of a year. Many new writers produce articles which sell, not for $25 or $50, but for $1,000 or more!

Your real problem isn't, "What can I make writing?" but rather, "How can I learn most quickly to produce salable articles?"

Once you have mastered these methods, you can sell the articles you write. Achieving success as an article writer results from an understanding of the techniques, familiarity with markets—and persistence.

Chapter II

THE MAGAZINE ARTICLE
MARKET

Is THERE anything a writer can do to shorten the period of apprenticeship required before he can produce salable magazine non-fiction? There is.

This does not mean that you may become a startling success overnight. Probably you can't. But if you are a man or woman of normal intelligence, you can learn in a few months to produce acceptable articles.

You begin right by working with hard facts, not with intangibles. And it is possible, even in this profession, to work with hard facts.

Your number one fact has to do with markets. What are the markets? What does each one want? Why? These are factors—material factors—in your success as a writer. And the sooner you learn these answers, the sooner you will be able to sell your articles.

TYPES OF MAGAZINES

Magazines are as different as women. And, like women —and men—each has a purpose. The editor will buy only articles which further the purpose of his publication.

It is apparent, therefore, that before you can write suc-cessfully for any magazine, you must understand that publication. To that end it is helpful to divide magazines into three general categories: Mass Circulation Magazines, Secondary Publications, and Small Magazines.

Mass Circulation Magazines

These publications—sometimes called general magazines—include such periodicals as *The Saturday Evening Post, Good Housekeeping, The Reader's Digest,* and comparable periodicals.

There is a relatively small number of mass circulation magazines. Some of them—*True, Esquire,* and *Playboy*—are men's publications; others—*Ladies' Home Journal, Good Housekeeping, McCall's*—are woman-interest books; and still others are aimed to interest both men and women.

Each of these magazines is a business. The objective of a publisher of this type of periodical is to make a profit. He hopes to do so through the sale of copies of his magazine and by the sale of advertising space.

These two are intimately related: The bigger the circulation of a periodical, other factors being equal, the more valuable the white space the magazine has to sell to advertisers. Therefore, the publisher seeks to build his circulation to the highest possible figure. How does he do this?

He does it by printing material which his readers will like well enough to make them buy the next issue of the magazine. As far as articles are concerned, this material consists of data that will help the reader. In some magazines this will be merely entertainment, in others it will be news, and in still others it may be self-help information.

All magazines in this category attempt to reward their readers by supplying them with valuable information.

The Reader's Digest, perhaps the world's most successful magazine, carries a notice each month that it seeks to publish articles of enduring significance. This is typical of the mass circulation periodicals.

It is understandable that such publications must demand high-quality manuscripts. Only by publishing such material can they reasonably expect to retain their high circulation. For this reason, these magazines pay fabulous prices for material. And, as a result, the competition among writers to sell editorial matter to the mass circulation publications is terrific.

There is, however, a happy facet to this situation: The magazines are always eager to find new writers who can produce potent articles. This includes the largest, most powerful publications.

What, precisely, do these magazines want in the way of non-fiction material? They want practically every type of literary material from the one-line epigram to the book-length manuscript. For instance, consider that stalwart among magazines, *The Saturday Evening Post,* Independence Square, Philadelphia, Pennsylvania.

In the feature class, it wants articles which will appeal to millions of readers. The range of subjects is wide— including sports, politics, international affairs, even profiles of towns and individuals. A typical issue contains the following articles:

"Why Do They Hate Us?"—an article dealing with anti-American riots in Panama.

"The Birds' Last Stand"—the story of a bird sanctuary at Stone Harbor, New Jersey, where more than 6,000 exotic birds have found a haven from the clamor of civilization.

"Pilots Aren't Obsolete"—a report pointing out that despite our missile-heavy defense program, the bomber is still an important element of national defense.

"Los Angeles' Cure for Drunks"—tells of a police rehabilitation farm in the California desert where alcoholics get plenty of hard work, good food, and sunshine.

"The Movies' Modern Marco Polo"—reports the story of Stanley Goldsmith, chief trouble-shooter for Twentieth Century-Fox, and his work throughout the entire world.

"They Call Me Madam"—the Perle Mesta story.

"Fabulous Mine in the Sea"—the story of the Grand Isle Sulphur Mine located seven miles out in the Gulf of Mexico.

"Touring Russia Made Easy"—an article telling that Russia has relaxed certain travel restrictions.

Who supplies all of this material for the *Post?*

According to the best available information, more than 85% of it comes from free-lance writers.

And what is the rate of pay?

"The prices we pay to individual writers are confidential," *Post* editors say, "but we can give you some idea of our general range.

"1. For a first article of normal *Post* length (4,000 to 5,000 words), we usually pay around $1,000, provided the author has not previously appeared in other major publications. If he is a well-known writer but has not previously written for us, the starting price of course will be considerably higher.

"2. Prices for articles from regular contributors probably will average around $2,250. Some of them get less than that and some get considerably more. We also pay most regular contributors for any expenses incurred in gathering the material in addition to the fee for the article itself.

"3. Prices for series material range all over the lot, depending on who writes it and who signs it and on the length. We often pay as much as $50,000 for the magazine rights to a non-fiction book-length manuscript, and this material usually will be packaged in the form of a series of six to eight parts. An autobiographical series by some celebrity often costs us far more than that. It is not unusual for us to pay the celebrity $75,000 or more for a six- to eight-part series, and, in addition, we usually have to pay a large fee to a collaborator."

Secondary Publications

Far too many writers feel that there is but one market for their literary wares—the mass circulation publications. This is a serious error. Another group of magazines buys thousands of articles each month.

The secondary publications include the general interest periodicals, regional magazines, and specialized magazines of many sorts, i.e.: *Arizona Highways, Today's Health, American Legion, Nation's Business, Successful Farming, Parents', Argosy, Woman's Day,* and hundreds of others.

These publications, too, are businesses. They must make a profit or cease to exist. Therefore, each editor is most interested in obtaining articles which will help him to build up the circulation of his magazine. This means that the editorial matter which goes into these publications must be first class. No editor in his right mind is going to publish an article unless he feels that doing so will help his publication. However, since these magazines pay moderate rates for manuscripts, you will experience far less

competition here than in the mass circulation field. The
result is that you stand a better chance to sell an article to
one of the secondary publications than to a big popular
magazine.

Just what kind of non-fiction do the secondary publications require? This depends upon the magazine. Perhaps
an illustration or two would be helpful. Let us look first at
Argosy, 205 East 42nd Street, New York, N.Y. Its non-
fiction fare in a typical issue includes:

"The Big Pull"—a story of the old-fashioned tug-of-war,
an especially rugged sport practiced by California lumber-
jacks.

"Broad Jumpers"—in Southern California almost any
week end you can find lassies in bikinis dropping from
the sky as man's last frontier falls prey to the fair sex.

"How to Add 30 Points to Your Score"—instruction by
America's top championship bowlers.

"We Crossed Africa by Outboard"—carting their boats
around raging cataracts, battling herds of hippos and war-
like natives, these explorers recorded one of the greatest
adventures of the century.

"Rough in the Saddle"—the story of pint-sized Manuel
Ycaza, a jockey who makes more enemies and wins more
races than any of his colleagues.

"I'll take Jamaica"—a travel story telling the delights
which await men in Jamaica.

And what is *Argosy's* attitude toward the free-lance
writer?

There is always a welcome mat out for the competent
writer at *Argosy.* "Our requirements," says Editor Henry
Steeger, "are sufficiently elastic to encompass practically
any type, any length, and any style story, provided that

it is of specific, hard interest to men and provided it is not in bad taste."

How good is the pay? Excellent. It usually runs around $500 for a feature article.

As an example of a secondary publication with woman interest, we may examine *Woman's Day,* 67 West 44th St., New York, N.Y. This is more than a monthly with woman interest. The editor beams it specifically at wives and mothers.

"Our articles," says Editor Eileen Tighe, "must be of help to the homemaker. This includes philosophy of living, rearing children, housekeeping, school, vacations. Our readers are interested in emotional and spiritual help, such as articles on faith, understanding and adjustment to life, etc. The chief requirements are straightforward honesty, sincerity, and usefulness to the reader."

This is the sort of article *Woman's Day* buys, as any issue will show. The issue before me as I write contains a lead article called "The Three Layers of Thankfulness," reporting the author's convictions about thankfulness. It is the kind of philosophy which parents may profitably pass on to their children as a part of the growing process.

Another article, "The Plight of the Program Chairman," is designed to aid the woman who must act as program chairman of the P.T.A. or some other local club. The author offers a number of practical suggestions which will be new to many, if not most, of the readers. Thousands of women can profit from reading this article.

"The Wing Chair" recounts what a certain piece of furniture has meant to the author down through the years. I should say that the objective of this article is to endear our homes to us, to make us a bit sentimental about them.

In "What Do You Mean, Normal?" the author states flatly that if we are to do the best we can, normal mustn't mean average. We should make strenuous effort to be healthy in body, mind, and spirit, to live up to the utmost of our human capacity. To be normal is not enough. Let's do better!

The foregoing, then, gives a clear-cut idea of the kind of articles *Woman's Day* wants to buy. It is, as Editor Tighe has said, material that is definitely helpful to the home-maker. And the more helpful the material, other elements being equal, the better your opportunity to sell the article.

What are the rates of payment?

Although *Woman's Day* has no set rate of payment, its rates are very good. More, it is a market in which both men and women may sell their wares.

Small Magazines

Another major division of publications—the Small Magazines—is quite different from the preceding ones. It includes the small daily newspaper, the weekly Sunday Supplements, juvenile magazines, religious periodicals, house organs, trade journals, and miscellaneous publications.

Thousands of these periodicals are not businesses at all in the ordinary sense. As a result, private companies send them free to millions of individuals.

Still another tremendous list of these magazines—the trade journals—goes to members of various trades—bakers, automobile mechanics, printers, restaurant owners, and members of every other trade and profession. Editors of these publications are eager to work with writers who demonstrate a comprehension of the publications' purpose and are willing to do enough research to produce valuable material.

Since there are thousands of small magazines—there are as many as fifteen or twenty devoted to a single industry —and the rate of pay is fair, it is not unusual for a skillful writer working in this field to earn an annual income of $20,000 or more.

And, finally, editors of these publications have little or no interest in "name" writers. Nor is the field overcrowded. Therefore, if you are wise, you will realize that the small magazine is the writer's best friend. It can become a minor gold mine.

Weekly and Small Daily Newspapers

Few beginning writers consider the small daily and weekly newspaper as possible markets. It is true that these are not major outlets for literary material, but they do buy news and feature articles. It is also true that you can find them in every part of the United States.

Your initial step in selling articles to this market is to obtain a few issues of those papers circulated in your community. You should study these, noting that they provide coverage for local sports events, police and court cases, huge fires, suicides, drownings, murders, traffic violations, and accidents resulting in death.

This, then, is grist for your mill. Your job is to get news of these happenings to the editor *before another writer does so*.

What training do you need in order to meet the demands of this market? Very little. Many correspondents for these papers are teachers, librarians, or just good citizens with a nose for news and a typewriter.

These men and women learn to gather facts—to be careful of their facts, and to write them in a brief, concise form, making sure that they include every important bit of information.

If you would sell to this market, you must be aware of what is going on in your community. You must know the church and school officials, the village and town boards, the fire department and police officials. You will keep in touch with the local lodges and clubs, the more influential citizens—including the politicians. These are your sources of information.

You must understand that the small newspaper, although paying very little for material, is a friendly market and, as a training ground for an aspiring writer, can become quite valuable. It well may lead you to larger newspapers, syndicates, and magazines.

Sunday Supplements

Practically all of the major newspapers have a Sunday magazine section. It may be called the "Magazine" or the "Sunday Magazine" or it may have a title such as *The Baltimore Sunday Sun Magazine, Detroit News Sunday Pictorial, Empire Magazine,* or *Today.* These magazines are known by the general name of Sunday Supplements.

Basically the Sunday Supplements want stories about unusual people residing in the territory in which the paper circulates. The Supplements also use articles about local points of interest.

"Local angles," says the editor of *Sunday,* a very good Supplement issued by the *Washington Star,* "are preferred, but subjects of broad interest are acceptable so long as the interest is universal."

In keeping with these criteria, Editor Love has published such articles as:

"A New Church in an Old Style"—the story of Trinity Episcopal Church at Upperville, Virginia, a building which may be compared architecturally to the Gothic cathedrals of Europe.

"Race Horse Painting for Race Horse Fans"—an article about John D. Schapiro, President of the Laurel, Maryland, race track, who has collected some 40 paintings portraying race horses and the racing scene.

"Crossing the River at White's Ferry"—an article telling of a picturesque ferry over the Potomac River in Montgomery County, Maryland.

And, in the unusual person category, Editor Love published an article entitled "Grandmas of the Rails," about two Maryland grandmothers who operate a "speeder" in the B & O yards at Brunswick, Maryland.

What should you write for your Sunday Supplement?

Your material should be timely. And it should be definitely local in subject matter. If your town has solved a problem of juvenile delinquency, has a "rock hound" who has become a skillful gem cutter, or has a resident who is a noted author or artist, probably your Sunday Supplement would be glad to see an article on this subject.

Most of the Sunday Supplements buy both text and photographs for illustrations. Your pay, therefore, may range from $25 to $100 or perhaps more for an illustrated feature in your local Sunday Supplement.

This is a market which is well worth your best efforts. You well may use it as a steppingstone to the big national Supplements such as *The Family Weekly, The American*

Weekly, Parade, and *This Week*—publications which pay handsomely, indeed, for acceptable copy.

Juvenile Publications

If you are a writer eager to sell copy in the shortest possible time, you must become acquainted with juvenile publications. These have been called the most important magazines in America today. This is because they play a major role in helping our oncoming generations to formulate their ideas.

These magazines are fundamentally different from the mass circulation and secondary publications in that juvenile periodicals do not exist to produce a dollar profit. Almost all of them have an entirely different purpose.

What is that purpose?

Before answering that question, I want to point out some major facts regarding juvenile publications. First, there are both secular and religious publications in the juvenile field. For instance:

Boys' Life, the Boy Scout publication, is secular. It is slanted to Boy Scouts.

Christian Youth, a publication of the American Sunday School Union, has a frankly religious appeal. "All of our material," says Editor William J. Jones, "must have evangelical Christian emphasis."

Yet, despite the fact that *Boys' Life* is secular and *Christian Youth* is religious, these two magazines are very close in purpose which we may state as:

To help readers become thrifty, industrious, intelligent, and honest—good American citizens.

The juvenile magazine, then, is a publication which has

as its chief purpose to build character in its readers. Editors who pass on the material which you submit consider your offering with this point of view: Will this manuscript help the readers to become upright, industrious, intelligent citizens? This, of course, is not the only consideration, but it is probably the most important of them all.

In order to make these magazines as effective as possible, publishers have divided them into five age groups as follows:

> Tiny Tots—3 to 6 years
> Intermediates—6 to 9 years
> Juniors—9 to 12 years
> Seniors—12 to 15 years
> Young People—15 to 18 years

The editor of each magazine knows the interests of his particular group of readers and selects material which has a definite appeal to the age group for which his magazine is edited.

Who finances these magazines? Churches and religious organizations publish most juvenile magazines. There are others which are published by special groups such as the Boy Scouts, Girl Scouts, and a few other organizations. Too, there are a few juvenile publications which are purely commercial, as is the case with the mass circulation and secondary publications.

It is worth noting that perhaps there are more magazines for a particular age group of juveniles than for any other class of individuals in the United States today. A writer friend of mine who specializes in this field recently told me that there are forty-three different markets for juvenile material in one age group alone!

Since most juvenile magazines pay relatively low rates for copy, you will have small competition in placing your articles in these publications. Moreover, once you have demonstrated a definite potential for juvenile writing, editors will gladly cooperate with you. Thus you can use juvenile magazines as a training ground for more lucrative writing. Many of today's well-known authors have made their first sales to juvenile publications. You can do the same.

Religious Magazines

One of the friendliest markets is the general, adult religious magazine. And, to the man or woman who is beginning to learn the profession of writing, a friendly market is a definite asset.

The religious magazines pay fairly well for their articles, and, in this market, you will have relatively little competition. Many of today's noted writers made their first sales to religious magazines.

But if you undertake to write articles for the religious periodicals, be sure that you comprehend their purpose. The editor must have material that fits the purpose of his magazine or it is totally useless as far as he is concerned.

"The religious writer's purpose," says Roland E. Wolseley, professor of Journalism at Syracuse University, "is to convey a religious attitude or point of view to the reader of or listener to his words. He is by function a propagandist, often even an evangelist . . ."

This is an extremely helpful statement. A writer who

sets out to produce an article which will convey a religious attitude or point of view is on his way to success.

There is a strong demand for the religious article. A writers' guide will list dozens of religious publications, outlining their editorial requirements. Moreover, even secular periodicals are using more and more religious articles. This is due, we are told, to an upswing in interest in religion in recent years. But whatever the reason, there is an increasing demand for forcefully written religious articles.

What should you write about?

Perhaps an illustration from a specific market will afford the best possible answer to this question. Therefore, let us consider the editorial needs of *Home Life*. This magazine carries a subhead reading "A Christian Family Magazine." Certainly this tells you that *Home Life* attempts to further the cause of Christianity and focuses its efforts on the family.

Editor Joe W. Burton is more specific. "We want," he says, "a contemporary picture of the best features of home life as it is lived today . . .

"Four elements are necessary in *Home Life* material: Christian in tone, related to family life, human in interest, and high in quality."

In an issue of that magazine on my desk appear the following titles: "I'm Glad I Married Him," "The Heart of a Child is a Rebel," "Worship at Our House," and "Teeners and Classroom Honesty." When you consider the purpose of this magazine, it becomes quite clear why Editor Burton bought these articles. They helped to further the purpose of his magazine.

If you want a friendly, uncrowded, big market—one well

worth your best efforts—give the religious magazines serious consideration. This well may lead to your first sales.

House Organs

"A house organ," reports *Gebbie Press House Organ Directory,* "is a publication issued on a regular basis by a company, firm, association, or even an individual that does not carry (outside) advertising, is sent free to readers, and —in one way or another—frankly promotes the interests of its sponsor." For instance: *Dodge News* published by Dodge Division of the Chrysler Corporation; *Municipal Construction* published by Armco Drainage & Metal Products, Inc.; *Plymouth Traveler* published by De Soto automobile dealers; *Friends* published by Ceco Publishing Company for Chevrolet car owners.

There are three general types of house organs. They are named according to the intended users as internal, external, or combination publications.

An internal house organ is designed primarily for the company personnel, an external for non-company personnel, and a combination is for both. The classification—internal, external, or combination—of house organ has a definite bearing on the type of copy it will use.

What types of articles do house organs use? "Subjects requested by editors cover nearly every topic under the sun," says Con Gebbie, the outstanding authority on this subject. "But it can be broken down, roughly, into these main categories:

"Women's fashions, men's fashions; beauty hints and aids; food features and recipes; sewing, patterns and how-to; care, feeding, and upbringing of children; home furnishings and decorations; appliances for the home from cellar to attic; general and technical book reviews; general and specific science features; home gardening and flower growing; outdoor sports including hunting, fishing, golfing, boating; home workshop tools, patterns, hints; general hobby features; cheesecake; the whole range of products information from general to the specific; travel articles, cartoons, and photographs."

It is reliably estimated that between 6,000 and 8,000 house organs are being published in the United States today, and most of them appear each month.

If you think these are unimportant publications, you could not be more wrong. In typography, layout, and general appearance they compare favorably with the mass circulation periodicals. Their circulation is more than 150,000,000—considerably greater than twice that of the combined circulation of all newspapers in the United States.

And if this looks to you like a first-class market, you couldn't be more right! That is precisely what it is.

Trade Journals

It may come as a surprise to you, but most writers completely overlook one of the largest literary markets. I refer to the business and trade magazines. Each industry has its own trade magazines—not just one, but anywhere from two to fifteen or twenty. There is a total of more than 5,000 of these magazines published in the United States today.

What is a trade journal?

It is a publication devoted to a given industry. It may be anything from a thin newspaper to a thick magazine printed on coated paper and illustrated in black and white and in color.

It circulates only among those interested in a given industry. For instance, *Boot and Shoe Recorder* goes to manufacturers, wholesalers, and retailers of the boot and shoe industry, not to consumers.

The basic function of the trade journal is to help the reader solve a particular problem so he may increase his profits. If the magazine can do this, the men in the industry will read it. And if that happens, the publication becomes a far more valuable advertising medium than it would be otherwise. Since advertising is the main source of income to trade journals—which are definitely controlled by the profit motive—editors really exert themselves to obtain truly helpful articles.

Each trade journal, therefore, strives to inform its readers, to help keep them abreast of the latest developments in their fields, to give them marketing information, news of new plants, new products, personnel changes, trade association meetings, and that sort of thing. If you can find a man who has made an outstanding success as a baker, a trade magazine dealing with the baking industry would very likely be interested in his story.

Perhaps you know a manager who took over a difficult job in the restaurant business but cleverly found happy solutions to all of his problems. By all means offer this story to a restaurant magazine.

What do these magazines use in the way of material?

Let us look at *Food Service,* one of the top trade journals in the restaurant field. The issue before me contains the following articles:

"Glamour Comes to Cafeteria Dining"—A completely

electric "wonder kitchen" speeds quality food to 1,000 customers daily in modern, quiet comfort.

"How Paper Service Can Save You Money"—Specific solutions to specific problems gathered from the accumulated experiences of food service directors all over the country.

"Convenience Foods on Dress Parade"—The secret ingredient in prefabricated foods is lower labor costs. With this in mind, the food service manager can let his imagination take wing, come up with some mighty fancy meals, and sell them at a greater profit.

"Put Public Relations to Work for You"—The "who, what and where" of a public relations program, written by an expert in the public relations field, stressing advertising and community relations.

"Design of Tomorrow's Drive-In"—A new drive-in concept based on a central commissary supplying streamlined outlets equipped with freezer storage and microwave ovens.

"He Took Business to Church"—Problems by the busload have been successfully solved by the manager of this unique cafeteria where lines of customers are often unbroken from 7:30 A.M. to 3:00 P.M.

Perhaps you feel that, in order to succeed as a trade paper writer, you must also be a successful businessman or woman. This is not true. A business background is helpful to a trade journal writer. But even that is not necessary.

You are a reporter. It is your job to find information which would be valuable to others in the trade, to present it in an interesting manner, and to illustrate it with appropriate photographs. That is all that is expected of you. And you can do this if you have never had a day's experience in the business.

How, then, does one go about getting into this interesting and wide open field?

First, you must learn what a particular publication wants to print. You may obtain this information from market guides, the professional journals, or from the magazines themselves. For instance: *Photo Developments* is a publication devoted to helping practicing photofinishers do a better job and make a bigger profit.

"We want case studies," says the magazine's editor, "of successful camera shops and successful photofinishing shops. Our readers are always interested in short cuts to production that save time and money and also in promotional ideas to build sales."

Like the big general publications, the trade magazines use photographic illustrations. "Articles for us," says Editor Heard, "must be illustrated by good photographs showing some special or attractive feature of the camera shop or finishing plant. More, the article itself must have been approved in writing by the shop owner."

Photo Developments will use articles of various lengths up to 2,500 words, or perhaps even longer in the case of an especially strong article.

The rate of pay at *Photo Developments* is 2½ cents a word and $5 a print for pictures. Many of the trade journals pay a much higher rate. The pay is good enough for many writers to devote their entire time to trade journals. Certainly these magazines are one of the best—if not the best—possible markets for the new writer.

The Writer's Best Friend

This chapter outlines in considerable detail the magazine non-fiction market today. To the beginning writer, the most important facet of this market is the small magazine.

The small magazine is the writer's best friend.

Therefore, you must learn the editor's specifications for articles. Be sure that you fully understand these—and this means you must begin with the publication's purpose.

Next, write the article to fit the editor's specifications. When you have done this, rest assured that the editor will, in response to your manuscript, give you a very satisfying check for that article.

Chapter III

WHAT IS A *GOOD* ARTICLE?

••

THE FACT that a magazine article which fits one periodical perfectly is totally unsuitable for another publication has puzzled many beginning writers. Just what is a *good* magazine article?

This is a basic question of great importance, and until you can answer it completely, you will make few, if any article sales. How can we distinguish between *good* and *bad* magazine articles?

First, a good magazine article must be suited to a particular periodical; it must contain ingredients which make it especially appropriate for a given audience. It is necessary, therefore, for you to understand what a magazine's readers want to read. Suitability is the first criterion for judging the sales possibilities of an article.

Each article reprinted in this chapter is designed for a specific publication—religious magazine, trade journal, or house organ.

RELIGIOUS MAGAZINE ARTICLES

The Leader is the outstanding religious magazine published by the David C. Cook Publishing Company. Although it is a religious publication, it is a commercial venture, a business, and is not subsidized in any way.

A professional-trade magazine for Sunday school super-intendents, department heads, and teachers, it needs ideas which these workers can apply to their own problems of teaching, staff recruitment, organization, planning, admin-istration, and good management.

"We do not want theory," says Editor Lucille C. Turner. "We want case history reports of workable plans which teachers and superintendents for all age groups are using in their Sunday schools. These should be unusual pro-cedures—methods which the average Sunday school worker may not have tried. The information should be docu-mented with names of people and places. Quotes help. Anecdotes are important."

Manuscripts for *The Leader* must not be generalized in content nor should they be pedantic and instructional in flavor. They must be written clearly and directly, sprinkled with illustrations and significant facts. Here is an example of one article they bought and published.

MEN'S BIBLE CLASS WORSHIPS IN WASHINGTON *

This month the Vaughn Bible Class of Calvary Baptist Church in Washington, D.C. celebrates its 70th anniversary. One of the world's oldest organized Bible classes, it has had a membership as high as 1,200 men! In this internationally fa-mous class congressmen, governors, cabinet members, at least one Chief Justice, and even a President of the United States have found inspiration and courage.

"How," you ask, "does this class appeal to men? How has it helped thousands of faithful members over the years? Just what is its secret?"

It has no "secret." But here is the way it does its job—with

* Reprinted by permission of *The Leader,* a David C. Cook publication.

plenty of take-home value for your church, too, regardless of size, denomination, or location.

As you might expect, a successful Bible class—like a profitable business—very often centers around an extraordinary individual. That was true in this case. The founder of the Vaughn Bible Class, Francis William Vaughn, was one of those devoted men—with an inspiring story, too.

At the Battle of Cold Harbor a bullet plowed into the young soldier's left arm. Gangrene developed and doctors warned of amputation. "Realizing my inability to cope with this ordeal," Vaughn said, "I carried my case to a higher court. I appealed to God. I made a solemn covenant with Him that if He would restore my arm, I would give my life to Christ." The arm healed and years later the war veteran—keeping his promise—organized the Vaughn Bible Class. Moreover, he poured himself into the undertaking to make it a thriving and inspiring affair.

The "Commander"—as Vaughn's friends admiringly called him—was an inspiration himself.

"The Bible was the Commander's meat and drink," said General William S. Shallenberger. "It became the infallible guide of his life, and the Holy Spirit led him into the homes and hearts of men."

Supreme Court Justice John M. Harlan paid high tribute to the man who did so much "to uplift the young men of the nation."

Vaughn was an inspiration—and a magnet! Churchmen turned out for his classes in all weather, and the attendance skyrocketed. But Vaughn was no grandstander. He wanted a *participating* Sunday school class and he got it. Pretty soon the Men's Bible Class was making its influence felt over Washington.

The class started an outstanding publication program. Generally, the publications have been issued weekly and distributed at the Sunday morning sessions but the class—maintaining that "Once a member, always a member"—also mails copies of its publications to members who have moved away from Washington.

The class undertook an aggressive membership campaign. It divided the city into several sections with a captain in charge of each. Captains checked up on the absentees and flung out a net for new members. The faithful captains and their lieutenants soon were dubbed the "Rain or Shine Club." One year the class sent out 1,000 invitation cards to prospective members. So the Vaughn Bible Class grew!

Next thing was to keep them coming and the Washington class provided big-name attractions—members had the opportunity to hear national figures lead Sunday school discussions. They still do today. Recently Congressman William Jennings Bryan Dorn of South Carolina talked to the class on Samuel. "The time was right," Congressman Dorn declared, "for a great leader in Israel. And Samuel was that leader. But that was not happenstance.

"Hannah, Samuel's mother," Congressman Dorn continued, "had prayed that God would give her a son. And in due time she bore a son and dedicated him to the work of God. She brought him up in the Temple of God."

Congressman Dorn concluded fervently, "I wish that modern parents would do the same."

As his class grew, Vaughn determined that it should have outreach. He called this a program for "The Other Fellow."

"The first step," Vaughn told his class, "is to get better acquainted. In the few minutes before the lesson, get the name of "The Other Fellow" nearest you and clasp his hand. Let him know that you are interested in him." It worked wonders! Vaughn himself became acquainted with every member of the huge class during its first quarter century. And he carried his efforts for "The Other Fellow" much further.

The churchman set aside Wednesday evening in his home to consult with his class members. He straightened out scores of difficulties, cheered hundreds of saddened hearts, and often helped in a material way.

This Christian concern was contagious. Dr. C. H. Dufour, for example, demonstrated his interest in "The Other Fellow" by offering to provide free medical service to any needy class member.

During the depression years, the Vaughn Class organized a Service Bureau to uncover jobs. The Service Bureau still operates, ministering to the physical needs and mending lives.

And that's the story of the Washington class. Still a livewire Christian service group today, seventy years later, Vaughn's prescription still holds, and should be the secret of a successful men's group in your church, too. To sum up:

1. See that you have a devoted, inspiring leader.
2. Make sure that your class participates—not just looks on and listens.
3. Reach out to recruit new members.
4. Plan a meaningful program.
5. See that you serve the other fellow!

Analysis

In your analysis of this article, you must begin with the fact that *The Leader* is designed to aid Sunday school classes to become bigger, more inviting to members and helpful to all concerned. This is its purpose.

Now you will observe that this article:

1. Tells the story of a really outstanding Sunday school class.
2. Begins with the promise of being interesting and helpful.
3. Reports pertinent details regarding the class founder.

4. Describes some of the methods by which the class grew to its present enviable stature.

5. Keeps moving from one intriguing incident to another, never become static.

6. Presents several new ideas—not theories but actual cases—which are workable in other classes.

7. Contains a considerable number of direct quotations.

8. Offers real inspiration.

9. Ends in a completely satisfying manner.

Furthermore, it is evident from reading this article that the writer, before putting a single word of the story on paper, thoroughly familiarized himself with the objectives of *The Leader*. He understood what that publication's readers hope to obtain from it. Then he searched for suitable material, set it down in readable form, and offered it to the editor. A few days later he was able to cash a sizable check for his effort.

This is the way a professional writer works. And this method points you to the most direct possible course for you to follow in your efforts to reap editorial checks for your manuscripts.

Trade Journal Articles

Now let us examine the editorial requirements of another magazine—one with a very different group of readers, *Photo Developments*. *Photo Developments* goes to a group of people devoted to operating camera shops and photo finishing studios. These men are skilled in their profession, but they are eager to learn more. And this is what the editor wants to give them—something that will show them how to improve their operation. The following article is an example:

TEAMWORK BUILDS MORALE AND SALES
FOR CROWN PHOTO*

What factors are essential for a successful photofinishing operation? If you ask officials at Crown Photo Service in Washington, D.C., they'll tell you that there are many, and that one of the most important of these is a close working relationship between management and production workers.

There are a number of ways in which this policy can be interpreted. Basically, it boils down to keeping employees happy in their work. And a survey of Crown's 200 employees quickly establishes this fact.

Maintaining top employee relations is no easy task, but it's one that pays off again and again. For this reason the management at Crown works constantly and diligently at this problem, attacking it from every possible angle.

For example, last year Crown made available to its employees preferred stock in the company. Now the participating personnel—approximately 80 percent of the total—are sharing in the company's ever-growing profits.

Still another healthy influence has been the forging of a closer contact between top management and supervisory personnel. This came about recently after one of the company's officers—secretary-treasurer Bud Schulman—attended the MPDFA's University of Illinois Management Institute. Upon returning to Crown, he resolved that its supervisors should exercise their full potential on the job. Therefore the company set up a series of classes designed to accomplish this.

The courses were swift-moving and covered a wide variety of pertinent topics, including: What employees want of their jobs; unions and their effect on present-day business; what management wants and expects of its supervisors; personnel rela-

* Reprinted with permission of *Photo Developments*.

tions with particular stress on good employee-company morale and how best to maintain it.

Each class was asked to solve in advance of a meeting a typical case problem which might be encountered in the course of any business day. Smaller discussion groups considered the answers to the problems presented. The case problems were general but served to point up the practical application of the principles being taught.

Greater understanding: The ending of these meetings was actually a beginning, or a point of departure. The supervisors gleaned a greater understanding of their own position in the role of management, of their responsibilities to their employers and their employees, and an insight into the policies of the company. Above all, they learned that their own jobs could be done more efficiently by delegating authority and by helping others.

The management of Crown Photo concluded from these sessions that a knowledge of good personnel relations can make the difference between a production worker and a supervisor. Communications between employees and management were markedly improved as the result of the course. In general, the program was highly successful and has led Crown Photo to urge other companies to follow suit.

There was a great deal of enthusiasm engendered by this thought-provoking course. In fact the supervisor's group asked for an extension of the program to be presented in four to six months. This would enable them to reaffirm their thinking in terms of pure mental stimulation.

Most of the supervisors commented that even after as many as fifteen years of supervisory responsibilities, they had never thought of their jobs in academic terms. Furthermore, they felt that such thinking provided them with a much better basis for making day-to-day decisions regarding the operation of their departments. So where Crown management had intended to provide a purely academic program, it turned out that the practical applications far outweighed the academic aspects of it.

An example of this awareness of supervisory responsibilities is reflected by a question asked by one of the supervisors as to whether the supervisor is a white collar worker or a blue collar worker in terms of job, dress, future, and attitude. The answer was, of course, that he is neither white collar nor blue collar worker but management.

Another morale-building Crown practice is to celebrate each employee's employment anniversary. This is the method: The employee's supervisor, in a little ceremony before the section personnel, presents the worker with a beautiful rose for each year of continuous service with the company. These occasions are greatly looked forward to.

Too, Crown has made its plants and offices pleasant places in which to work by the installation of air conditioning and soft music. In addition, there is a Swing Room where employees may go for lunches, drinks, or relaxing.

Another management technique which Crown utilizes is the Junior Board idea. Every supervisor at Crown is a member of this Board which shares the responsibility for effective management progression. The Board meets once a month for informational discussions of various operations and policies, thereby enabling each supervisor to familiarize himself with other phases of the company's operations.

In addition to making the organization more closely knit and effective, these meetings serve as training ground for those who aspire to assume more responsible positions.

Of course there are other essential ingredients that contribute to the success of Crown Photo Service. Serving outlets within a 175-mile radius of Washington with both color and black-and-white finishing, the company is equipped to process in excess of 1,000 rolls of film per hour. And as might be expected, there is considerable emphasis on quality control.

Basic in this Master Member's system of quality control is its filtered water system. Using as much as 2,500,000 gallons of water during a peak summer month, the firm maintains its own filtration plant and a 500-gallon glass storage tank. In addition to the constant supply of pure water, heating and chilling units assure that the water is always maintained at the correct temperature levels for best processing results.

Moreover, the firm is continually making an effort to improve its techniques. As an example, Crown uses the Retouch-a-Print system for reducing makeovers. This method of further developing light prints by hand before they pass into the short-stop is advertised to the public as one more way in which Crown Photo is striving to give the customer the best in quality —and it has paid off.

Cutting Costs: Keeping costs down is always an important consideration. And Crown has greatly reduced advertising and printing costs since the acquisition of a Multilith machine and a good operator to run it. Now the firm produces all of its own stuffers, direct mail advertising pieces, stationery, and forms.

Tracing lost orders has been greatly simplified through the use of a 5x8-inch card form on which is listed the dealer number of the missing order, the date that film was submitted, and the customer's name, address, and telephone number. This form is designed to fit like a regular processing envelope into the dealer's uncalled-for photo finishing file.

When a complaint is received about an undelivered order, Crown sends this form to the dealer who placed the order for the customer. On the card is printed: "A complete search is in progress for the above customer's order. Everything possible is being done to locate it at an early date. Please extend our sincere apologies for this delay." Beneath is space for the dealer's name.

Crown Photo Service, a closed corporation, is controlled by four families which founded it. The founders are: Harry Schulman, George Cullen, Tony Ludwig (now retired) and Jim Sullivan.

The basic day-to-day operation is the responsibility of four of the founders' sons: Charles Cullen, plant manager; Don Ludwig, in charge of sales, advertising, and dealer personnel training; Kenneth Ludwig, who handles special projects; and Bud Schulman, secretary-treasurer.

In commenting on the example set for them by their fathers, Bud Schulman says, "The advice of our experienced elders over the years has meant much to us." And from the progressive operation of this company, it is certain that Crown's sales will continue to make the steady climb that has seen them rise from $325,000 in 1946 to more than $3,000,000 in 1957, a tribute to the healthy company atmosphere of good employee relations.

Analysis

You need to do little analyzing to understand why this article sold. It is packed with data which has materially aided Crown Photo Service to become one of the nation's leaders—if not the leader—in this highly competitive field. Those tips will help others in the business.

Help is the key word. When you offer a trade magazine editor a manuscript containing specific information by which those in the business can profit, you will make a sale. And the better your suggestions, other elements being equal, the bigger your check will be.

Specifically, what help does this article give the reader? Let us enumerate some of the points:

1. It aims to interest one specific group of people—photofinishers.

2. It gives policies, practices, and procedures used by

one of the greatest—if not the greatest—company of its kind in the world. This is expert testimony.

3. It points out several means of obtaining and retaining good employee relationships—methods which other photo developers may utilize in their shops.

4. It explains how to make the personnel do a better job—how these same individuals may advance to better positions.

5. It describes a morale-builder—the celebration of the employee's employment anniversary.

6. It tells the story of Crown's Swing Room, its use, and the results of it.

7. It explains how Crown handles the pure water problem, something that is of real interest to every photo finisher.

8. It mentions how Crown manages to give a better print—via the Retouch-a-Print system.

9. It tells how Crown goes about tracing lost orders. This shows how Crown handles an important public relations problem.

10. It shows how Crown saves money on forms, stuffers, stationery, and the like.

Here, then, is information that is valuable to the photo finishing world. Small wonder the article sold!

Just remember this in preparing a story for a trade journal, the purpose of the publication is to aid its readers in making money more pleasantly and efficiently. Therefore, your job as a writer is to produce precisely that kind of material. And when you do that, you need not worry about sales. They will surely care for themselves.

HOUSE ORGAN ARTICLES

Now let us try an experiment. Suppose you find an attractive magazine, one for which you feel you could produce articles, but you are unable to locate market tips explaining what the editor wants to buy. This is a real life situation.

What do you do?

Perhaps an illustration would be helpful. Your magazine, let us say, is *Success Unlimited,* an excellent small magazine.

When you look this magazine over rather carefully, you discover that Napoleon Hill Associates, a division of the W. Clement Stone Enterprises, is the publisher. W. Clement Stone, you read, is President of Combined Insurance Company of America, Hearthstone Insurance Company of Massachusetts, Combined American Insurance Company, First National Casualty Company, and General Manager of Napoleon Hill Institute.

You find on the masthead a significant line—"The monthly magazine for self-improvement." This, you decide, harmonizes with the title of the magazine, *Success Unlimited.* These facts seem to indicate to you that *Success Unlimited* is an optimistic magazine, a positive magazine which deliberately plans to encourage its readers to push forward to great and still greater achievements.

Skimming the magazine, you find several articles, including:

"Put Honor First"—Whether you are playing football or selling hardware, running for political office or trying a case in court, no victory is worth the price if it costs your integrity.

"Is Your Wife a Future Financier?"—Husbands who

maintain that women can't manage money would be severely criticized by the banks of America. Surprised bankers recently discovered that women are their best customers.

"The Sales Formula that Never Fails"—untold secrets in the art of selling.

"Your Pathway to Success"—telling how men and women may utilize their greatest resources.

This preview gives you a fairly accurate idea of what *Success Unlimited* wants in the way of articles. But you will want to read a full article like the following one and analyze it before coming to a conclusion.

STOP CHEATING YOURSELF *

By Omer Henry

Are you a bit bored with life? Is there a deadening monotony to your days, a restlessness to your nights? Do you wish to Allah that you could break away and, just once, do something a bit interesting?

Thousands of folk who felt this way are filling their days with eagerness for the next hour, achieving a wide range of highly desirable objectives, ballooning their happiness to unexpected and eminently satisfying magnitudes.

There is nothing secret about their methods. "Your first step toward breaking the dullness of your days," says Jack Davis of San Francisco, "is to decide on an objective. Mine? I wanted to restore antique cars."

Davis bought a 1917 Maxwell. When he had it running well, he sold it and bought a 1909 Firestone Columbus, a really rare car. "It gives me a terrific bang," he says, "to take a heap of junk and make it run like a limousine."

What can a woman do? Mildred T. Johnstone of Bethlehem, Pennsylvania answered that question with needle, thread, and fabric. Choosing the steel industry as the subject for needle-point paintings, she so perfected her art that colleges, craft museums, and art galleries—even in foreign countries—have asked her to stage exhibitions of her works.

"What a pleasant way," a friend remarked to her, "to pass your time."

"That," Mrs. Johnstone replied, "is precisely what I am not doing. Instead, I'm animating time by filling it with positive living."

Her method contrasts sharply with that of Elizabeth Stuteville of Alfalfa, Oklahoma. A high school teacher, she went to the same classroom every school day in the year, met the same students, taught the same subjects, heard the same answers.

In the afternoons, she prepared dinner for her husband, son, and herself. Then she washed dishes, planned the next day's work, and began the routine all over again.

The monotony was maddening. How could she get real interest into her life? If she could just take a trip to New York and—

Trip to New York? Why not? For her senior class? They'd love it and it would give her something interesting to plan.

She discussed her idea with rancher Arlo King who agreed to convert his cattle truck into a "pullman on rubber." By the time the truck was ready for the trip, its van-like interior suggested part of a comfortable home. Near the cab several plastic bags filled with clothing hung from a steed rod. Above it a radio loudspeaker promised hours of entertainment as the class rode along.

The party visited Oklahoma City, Memphis, and Washington. Then, on a Friday afternoon, it entered New York.

After seeing the Empire State Building, Madison Square Garden, Broadway, Wall Street, the Bowery, Chinatown, and the United Nations, the party proceeded to Niagara Falls, across into Canada, and returned to the United States at Detroit.

The 16-day trip for the party of 13 cost $1,020—the travel bargain of the century. But of far greater importance, Mrs. Stuteville found a way to make the entire school year fascinating for herself, the senior class, and the Alfalfa community.

Working in a somewhat similar manner, Paul Hagenbuch, an east coast machinist, found a way to enliven his days. "All my life," he says, "I wanted to travel. It happens that my wife shares my ambition." The trouble was the cost. How could Paul finance such trips as he and his wife would like to make?

He worked out an original solution—a housecar—which is neither an automobile nor a trailer but a combination of both. As his initial step, he removed the trunk door, a portion of the top, and the rear seats from a 1949 Buick sedan. Using steel rods he constructed a framework extending approximately six feet from the car's floor.

When the frame was in position, Paul weatherproofed it with aluminum, installed a shower with hot and cold running water, a kitchen sink, small electric range, an insulated food chest, and a double bed suspended from the ceiling. The complete job is large enough to house the Hagenbuchs comfortably for weeks, even months.

Another man, Hezzy West, a welder, added zest to his life in a different way. Born in Gainesville, Florida, he worked for years with boats. Later, completely divorced from the sea, he settled down in Glen Echo Heights, Maryland.

He missed his boats. "I wanted a cabin steamboat," he says, "and I didn't even have a birchbark canoe."

What did he do? "I bought me some steel plate, angle irons, and beams for a boat. Then I thought how I wanted her to look. And when I had her well in mind, I laid the keel for a 30-footer and built her right up from there."

Not only did Hezzy build the steel hull, square cabin, smoke funnel, and bilge pump. He also built the boat's two steam engines.

Hezzy's boat, the *Northwind,* cost him, aside from his labor, the amazingly low sum of $350. It's a safe bet that, when piloting the *Northwind* down the Potomac, Hezzy feels as if he has a lease on heaven. And why not? The seaworthy *Northwind* is the envy of a hundred men who own and operate far more expensive boats.

Donald E. Callar of Alexandria, Virginia breaks the routine of his job by building precision rifles and loading his own ammunition. A lathe in his workshop helps him fashion the prize winning barrels of his masterpieces.

The evening I visited him, he was reloading .30-30 shells. In weighing the powder, he was as careful as a master pharmacist compounding a potent prescription.

Using his own guns and ammunition and competing with nationally renowned experts, Callar often wins a handsome portion of the prizes at benchrest meets.

Under the circumstances it is hardly surprising that Callar finds every minute of his day fascinating. His secret? "I do something in which I am intensely interested."

How can people do all of these marvelous things? Where do they get the time?

A recent survey shows that the average American workman's annual leisure runs to the amazing total of 2,200 hours—approximately 200 hours more than he works!

It is clear, therefore, that each of us has ample time for a full, rich, and satisfying life. You can within reasonable limits do anything you really want to do.

If you are permitting your days to pass as routine, dull, and uninteresting, you're short-changing yourself on life's most im-

portant element—and without cause. To make your life fascinating is entirely within your power.

It's high time for you to wake up and live. Stop cheating
yourself!

Analysis

Who reads *Success Unlimited*? Mature people who wish
to get ahead in life.

"Our editorial needs," says William H. Meyers, Executive Editor, "are stated most succinctly in the statement
that *Success Unlimited* magazine is published 'to help the
reader to help himself to more of the good things of life.'

"We are looking for articles of a self-help, how-to, inspirational, or spiritual nature with a strong 'you' slant so
the reader can relate the text directly to himself. Such
articles might show the reader how to solve problems,
learn to work more efficiently, win raises or promotions,
live more happily, enjoy a better family life, etc."

What did the writer of "Stop Cheating Yourself" give
the reader? A bit of study will reveal the following do-
nations:

1. Knowledge that others are getting a lot out of life,
men and women who have plenty to do on the job, at
home, or both.

2. Inspiration. This article shows that you, the general
reader, if you really want to do so, can improve your lot
considerably.

3. Suggestions as to what you may do toward improving
your own happiness. There are many of them. One man
reconditions old cars, a woman does needlepoint art work,
and one man makes precision rifles. These are activities in
which the readers, if they so desire, may indulge.

4. A selling point. The really big point about this arti-

cle is the fact that the average American today has leisure of 2,200 hours annually—200 hours more than he puts in on the job! That is enough to bowl over most readers. It is a forceful rebuttal to the man or woman who says, "Oh, I'd love to do this, but I don't have the time." The indisputable fact is that all of us have the time. But it is only those who use their time wisely who get along well.

This, incidentally, is new information to most readers of *Success Unlimited*.

5. And from this article one can well understand that there is real substance to *Success Unlimited*. Its philosophy is positive, constructive, hopeful, and courageous.

Too, the complete analysis of this article will include the consideration of its presentation. Look at it from that point of view for a moment.

In "Stop Cheating Yourself," the title commands attention. That is the author's initial bid to reader and editor for a full reading. In effect, these three words say, "Mr., you probably are cheating yourself. And there's no point to it. Why not read the truth here and improve your situation?"

But this is only the beginning. In the lead paragraph, the author writes: "Are you a bit bored with life? Is there a deadening monotony to your days, a restlessness to your nights? Do you wish to Allah that you could break away and, just once, do something a bit interesting?"

Do you find that intriguing? The author meant it to be. He hoped that you would read on to the next paragraph to find out how you could improve your lot.

The author, however, was not quite ready to let you go on your own at this stage in the article. He felt that this article needed direction. And so he wrote:

"Thousands of folk who felt this way are filling their days with eagerness for the next hour, achieving a wide range of highly desirable objectives, ballooning their happiness to unexpected and eminently satisfying magnitudes."

Now, according to this author, there is nothing secret about the methods these people use. And he proceeds to give a generous set of rather interesting examples.

And finally he comes to the end of the story. "It is clear, therefore," he writes, "that each of us has ample time for a full, rich, and satisfying life. You can, within reasonable limits, do anything you really want to do.

"If you are permitting your days to pass as routine, dull, and uninteresting, you're short-changing yourself on life's most important element—and without cause. To make your life fascinating is entirely within your power.

"It's high time for you to wake up and live. Stop cheating yourself!"

And that, I think you will agree, is a forceful and fully satisfying end for this article.

"But this analysis," you say, "looks like work."

Brother, you are right. It is work. But it produces results. And that is what we are after.

By following this plan you can come to a rather definite understanding of what any magazine wants to publish. Once you know that, you have helped yourself as if with seven-league boots toward selling your editor not one but many articles. When you put into practice the principles outlined in this chapter, you are well on your way to producing not only good articles but articles that are good for a particular market—articles that will sell.

Chapter IV

CONCEPTION OF AN ARTICLE

•••

YOUR INITIAL action in writing a magazine article is to get an idea—a valid idea—for an article. And don't let the word "idea" frighten you. There is nothing mysterious about it. An idea is simply a subject. It may be as prosaic as How to Plant Beans or as romantic as The Best Way to Make Love.

How do you get an idea? The answer is simplicity itself: You learn through market tips and by reading the magazine you wish to write for what the publication uses. Then you select a suitable subject. That is your idea.

SOURCES OF IDEAS

In looking for article ideas, you may begin with the newspapers. Not long ago, for instance, the Washington *Star* reported the completion of a new kind of garage. According to the item, this innovation was an entirely automatic operation—the only one of its kind in existence. With this system, a car could be whisked from the ground floor into its parking stall on the eighteenth floor of the new building in less than sixty seconds, undoubtedly making this the world's speediest garage. Being a push-button garage, it required only one attendant. Given this information and a knowledge of the editorial needs of *Munici-*

pal Construction, you could see that here was an idea for an article for that magazine.

Writers everywhere find the newpaper a fruitful source of magazine article ideas, a veritable gold mine. Use it!

Even a roadside sign may give you an idea for a magazine article. Recently I saw a sign, in no way dramatic or outstanding, which read: *Eagle Aerie 1311.*

Those words refer to the lodge hall in Morristown, New Jersey of the Fraternal Order of the Eagles, an organization which publishes a fine fraternal periodical. I happened to know that the editor likes to print in each issue of *Eagle* magazine a story of a different aerie. As I noted the sign, I thought that perhaps here was an idea for an article for *Eagle.* Stopping to make some inquiries, I found that Aerie 1311 was almost as old as the Order itself. One of the charter members of the aerie was still living—had been an active member of the lodge for more than half a century. Too, the aerie had just moved into its new and very attractive hall which was fully equipped with a game room, lodge hall, kitchen, and all of the many things which go to make a fraternal clubroom outstanding.

And back of this, Morristown was a most historic city, still tingling with fascinating tales of the Revolutionary War.

I developed this idea into an article and the editor of *Eagle* bought it immediately. The roadside sign was an idea that had paid off handsomely.

The source of another idea was a parked Ford truck. As its body design was different from any I had seen, I stopped to examine it. Noting that the truck carried the familiar

Pepsi-Cola colors and markings, I called the local Pepsi dealer and talked to him about the truck.

"Yes," he said, "the truck is a special design. In fact, I designed it. There is no other like it. I use it particularly in transporting vending machines. Its low platform bed makes the loading and unloading of these machines far easier than is the case with any other truck."

This, it appeared to me, was an idea for an article for *Clues,* an excellent magazine which goes to Ford truck users. I made a few additional inquiries and learned where the dealer got the idea for the body design, how he built it, and how well it served the purpose for which it was intended. I learned why he used a Ford truck. Next, I took a few action pictures, in black and white and in color, showing the various uses of the truck. At home the following day I set about turning my material into cash. I turned one angle of this material—that featuring the Ford truck—into an article that sold to *Clues* for a thoroughly satisfying check.

Still I had more material. What about an article for *Vending,* the trade magazine for vending machine operators? I wrote that article, offered it to *Vending,* and a few days later had a second check for one idea.

Another excellent source of ideas for magazine articles is the activities of local groups of one kind or another. For instance, recently the First Baptist Church of Alexandria, Virginia staged what is called a Laymen's Conference on Christian Living.

This was something of an innovation in the field of church activity. The theme of the conference was: The successful business or professional man practices Christianity. And the conference brought in a number of noted Christian business and professional men to give expert testimony on this subject.

When I heard of this meeting, it appeared to me that here was an idea a small magazine might use as the basis of an article. After making enough inquiries to give me a fair idea of what market would be interested in this material, I decided *Success Unlimited* would buy a compact, hard-hitting, genuinely helpful article on this subject.

Recalling that *Success Unlimited* uses spiritual material and goes to businessmen, I accumulated detailed data as to what happened at this conference. Next, I wrote the article, and offered it to *Success Unlimited*. I did not have to wait long for a narrow slip of green paper which my bank gladly exchanged for coin of the realm.

What, then, are your sources of ideas for salable magazine articles? The chance remark of a friend, a new statue, a church or school project, a community activity, a special event, a national holiday. These are but a few; actually, your sources are infinite. They are all around you—more than you could possibly use if you were to live ten times as long as Methuselah.

Your real problem is not "Where can I find ideas" but "Which ones should I develop?"

EVALUATING ARTICLE IDEAS

Here are some questions that you should ask to help you evaluate the ideas which occur to you:

1. Is this material worth publishing? Would it actually help readers? Can you cram into it enough helpfulness to make the reader really glad the magazine published it? If you can honestly answer all of these questions in the af-

firmative, probably your idea is worth putting into an article.

2. How much travel would this entail? It costs time and money to travel to those alluring spots far away, and frequently when you arrive you are disappointed. Start your article writing with subjects near at hand.

3. What will a magazine pay for this material? If you are wise, you will work for the publication that will pay most for your time and effort. You will learn from statements in market tips and from actual experiences with editors that some magazines pay infinitely better than others. And you will also learn that competition is greater in the higher-paying books.

4. How much research would it be necessary for you to do in producing a given article? Let's assume, for instance, that you know of a church that has just completed a project that would make a good article for *The Leader*. However, you also know that the only time you've been inside a church in the past twenty years was when your cousin married the son of the Methodist preacher at Sugartown.

Therefore, it is obvious that before you could write an article that would be convincing to the editor of *The Leader*, you'd need to do a considerable amount of research about churches, their methods of operation, and the like. You could do this, but the problem is: Would you make more cash per hour doing this research or by writing for a publication dealing with golf, a subject which you know thoroughly?

5. What about illustrations? Almost all of the small magazines require photographs for illustrative purposes. If you can supply them, you will augment the size of your

check. Your problem then becomes: Where can I get suitable photographs? What will they cost? What would be the profit to me for getting them? You will, of course, choose to do the article that will *net* you the most cash.

6. What are the possibilities of re-using this material? If you can make one research job do for two or three articles, you will be saving time for yourself. Time plus effort equals cash, so in selecting ideas to develop, you may want to consider whether a given subject can be slanted in more than one direction.

7. How timely is this article? You will find that timeliness helps to sell an article. Therefore, the astute writer produces timely articles and submits them to publishers well in advance of the suitable publication date.

For most weekly magazines such copy should be submitted from four to six weeks in advance of date of publication; three to six months for the monthlies.

8. How many people are interested in this material? Other elements being equal, an editor will favor an article that would intrigue a million readers over one that would appeal to but half that number.

9. How strong is the appeal of this material? Some subjects—sex, money, taxes—have a very strong appeal to almost every adult. Other subjects—the glories of ancient Rome, the romance of Venice, the desirability of owning one's own home—have much weaker appeal to most readers.

10. How much has already been written on this subject? Obviously, you will stand a better chance to sell an article on a subject that has not been written and rewritten a thousand times. You can help yourself to select appropriate ideas by keeping abreast of developments in

your spheres of interest. That is, if you write on salesmanship, be sure you are aware of the latest methods of selling.

If you write of family life, read regularly what the authorities are advocating. Learn the results of surveys, ex-
periments, and investigations. Armed with such information, you will be in a position to select ideas which your
readers will be eager to see developed.

When you do that, you will find editors writing to you,
asking you for more articles. And selecting the right ideas
is a big step in that direction.

NOTES AND NOTEBOOKS

You will want to adopt a plan of keeping on hand a
good supply of ideas for ready use. This means that you
must record those which you feel are suitable to develop
into articles.

The simplest possible way to do this is by using a notebook. A stenographer's notebook, because of its handy
size and heavy cardboard covers, is ideal for this purpose.
Also, you will find it timesaving to make your idea notes in
longhand.

These notes must be brief. Here are some taken from
my notebook:

Freedoms Foundation. This is an organization about
which I have considerable information. I have written two
articles about it, but it is worth still others. These two
words are enough to keep me from forgetting the idea.

Report cards—how they are marked today. This is
enough to call to my mind that there is a strong feeling
that present day report cards are too vague, that they fail
to reveal a child's shortcomings or give him adequate
credit for excelling in certain subjects.

Sometimes I note after an idea the name of a magazine which I feel may be interested in a particular idea.

There are other methods of recording ideas. One is to use a 3x5 card for each idea, give it a title, and file it in a special Idea File.

Another method utilizes a letter-size Manila folder. Into it you place clippings taken from newspapers and magazines—clippings containing ideas which you may wish to develop into articles at a later date. These plans really help the serious writer.

"Within six months after I started this (card file for ideas) system," said one article writer, "I had a bulging stack of cards—article leads—filed under about a dozen different classifications, such as grocery, drug retailing, garages, fishing, and so forth. Whenever I want to do a story, all I have to do is to riffle through this lead file. I always find something interesting and so will you, if you use this method."

You will find such a plan indispensable if you really intend to write for money. Writing for money is a business, and if you treat it as one, your checks will come more easily and with a satisfying frequency. Recording your article ideas will help—materially.

Using Ideas Successfully

However important the preceding suggestions may be —and they are tremendously important—they must all give way to this one: *Using Ideas*. This, by all means, is the most significant aspect of successful article writing. In other words, what you do with the idea is infinitely more helpful in selling the article than the idea itself. It is imperative that you develop your idea in a professional manner if you hope to make a sale.

How do you develop an idea in the professional manner? Perhaps the best answer is an example, in this case from *Pen* magazine.

First, we must understand *Pen*'s editorial needs. *Pen* is a monthly magazine for the Federal Postal Employees Association, government employees and public servants. It uses general and family interest articles up to 2,500 words in length. From this we may know that *Pen* readers are men and women interested in their homes, families, and careers. It is unlikely that they have been involved in serious trouble.

Now, what kind of idea would appeal to this audience? What about children—delinquents? Do you think *Pen* readers would be interested in knowing how they may keep their children from becoming delinquents?

Writer Harris Hartmann felt that this was a suitable idea for *Pen* magazine. It so happened that he had information about a teacher—Red Henderson—on the west coast who had been remarkably successful in handling children. But before Hartmann began writing this article, he did some thinking. "How," he asked himself, "can *Pen*'s readers profit from what Henderson did with these kids in his classes?"

Too, Hartmann considered methods by which Henderson had achieved outstanding success. This information, Hartmann decided, would make the article quite useful to *Pen* readers. And finally, Hartmann asked himself, "What is the big thing—the selling point—in my article?"

This was not too difficult to answer. The record proves conclusively that Henderson's ideas really work.

"These facts," Hartmann concluded, "put my article out of the realm of theory. My story is true. Henderson's method produced the desired results."

The natural conclusion for a reader to form, having had these facts presented, is that since Henderson's methods worked for him, there is good reason to believe they will work for the reader. That is an important selling point in an article. It offers real help to the reader. And that is precisely the thing he is attempting to find—help. Before Hartmann began to write his article, he deliberately considered the elements which a *Pen* reader would find valuable. When all of this was done, he wrote the article. Here it is; read it to see how Hartmann developed his idea.

AN OUNCE OF PREVENTION *

By Harris Hartmann

Juvenile arrests in the United States are increasing at an alarming rate. In 1957 they rose 10.8% over that of 1956. "This fact," says J. Edgar Hoover, Director, Federal Bureau of Investigation, "reflects our tragic failure to cope with the situation."

What is to be done about this? Thoughtful men and women throughout the country are giving this matter serious attention.

"What is it," they ask, "that makes one teen-ager turn to violence, another become an inspiration to his family and the community in which he lives?"

Red Henderson, physical education instructor in the Spokane, Washington, Public Schools, feels that he has, at least, a part of the answer. For several years he has been trying out his theory and with most gratifying results.

It all began in 1947 when Red agreed to give a few of his

* Reprinted by permission of *Pen* magazine and the author.

pupils some extra square dance sessions. This little group became the Silver Spurs, one of the most unusual youth organizations in the nation. It consists of boys and girls whom Red has made into a band of dance specialists.

These ordinary kids from average homes are intelligent, do not drink or smoke, are cooperative, loyal to their school and each other, and unconceited. Usually they are outstanding in church, civic, and scouting affairs.

One may become a member of this select group only by being elected to it. Every high school student in Spokane has that opportunity but, as the group is small, only those with the highest number of votes are accepted.

For the lucky ones the winter months are filled with much hard work. Red devotes considerable time and effort to preparing authentic costumes, training the Silver Spurs in new dances, and staging local dance programs.

These are by no means ordinary dances. For instance, the Silver Spurs repertoire, with the lovely waltzes, mazurkas, and polkas of the antebellum South, the Scandinavian Northwest, and the Spanish Southwest, is unusually complete.

Amazed spectators may see besatined Colonials return from before the Revolution for the quadrilles such as The Lancers or contras like The Beaux of Albany or cotillions—perhaps The Carnival Square Dance, popular with our French Colonists 300 years ago.

Yet still to come are the popular cowboy square dances, some of them already more than a century old before they went West with the covered wagons, the humorous Philippine Bamboo Dance which imitates the silly twinkling bird of Leyte, hopping from branch to branch so it will not get its feet wet, and the ever-exciting American Indian dances—the War Dance of the Northwest, the Indian Hoop Dance of the Southwest, the Butterfly Dance and the Owl Dance.

Fifteen hundred years roll back when the Silver Spurs dance

the Matlanchines, even as the Aztecs once did while black-robed priests offered the still pulsing heart of a sacrificial victim to the setting sun.

Every dance has its own significance, and costumes valued at more than $30,000 lend color and charm to all of them.

The winter months, however, are only a prelude to the vacation time. Each June, in a chartered bus under Red's supervision, the Silver Spurs start out on a several-thousand-mile tour.

It is a very special trip. Red has arranged the itinerary with great care, accepting only the sponsorship of uncommercial and recognized community, church, educational, and public service organizations. On tour Red billets the kids by two's in private homes of the sponsoring agencies.

The Silver Spurs have two programs of about 40 dances which they alternate when on the road. And here is the heart of their success. When they dance, they are not performing; they are telling people of today about the life and times of those invisible ancestors whose ethics and manners are inherent in these traditional dances.

"Our favorite engagements," Red says, "are those given in a school gymnasium big enough for everyone to join in a big square dance as the last part of the entertainment."

Dancing, according to Red, is only half the fun of the tour. Seeing America is even more important. "Every museum, historical site, and national shrine," he says, "becomes a place of excitement to fill young minds with memories and to fire imaginations with visions of greatness.

"The sights the kids see, coupled with the history they learn from their dances, give them not only an understanding of the American way of life but a strong sense of the responsibilities of such a heritage."

It is hardly surprising that Red has been outstandingly successful in his work with the Silver Spurs. A graduate of the

State College of Washington, he is a recognized authority on American dances—particularly the square dance.

When other experts find themselves stumped by the intricacies of a newly discovered dance—one with a name like "Fencin' in the Prairie Hen" or "The Yuciapa Twister"—they ask Red about it. Invariably he draws out, with mathematical precision, the dance's routine, its steps, and recites the words of its "call" for them.

Under Red's supervision the Silver Spurs have enjoyed a succession of spectacular successes. They have appeared on more than a thousand stages, on radio, and TV.

But that is not all. The Standard Oil Company of California has made a 30-minute color film of these boys and girls in action. As a part of its public service education program, the Company makes this film available for showings all over the country.

Nor is that the end of the Silver Spurs' fame. It has even become international, for the United States Information Agency has sent this story, complete with text and pictures, to 77 foreign countries. In short, these boys and girls have had more favorable publicity than an average Congressman in a full term of office. And they deserve it all!

"And," Red says with fully justifiable pride, "not one of the Silver Spurs has become a juvenile delinquent. This is because we have displayed a real interest in them, their problems, associates, and the activities which occupy their spare time. *That is the key to keeping youth out of trouble—show genuine interest in them.*

"Youth," he adds, "is terribly maligned. Too many adults engage in this sort of thing as a pastime. They stigmatize modern youth as unruly, dangerous, and predisposed to delinquency.

"Nothing could be farther from the truth. There are delinquent juveniles, of course. Too many of them. But today's teen-agers are smarter, more self-sufficient, and more constructive than at any other period in our history.

"We can help them most by really taking an interest in them and their activities. The ounce of prevention, you know."

Looking back on Red's record, it seems that he has a substantial point because not one of the Silver Spurs has become involved in any difficulty with the law. Instead, when one of them gets out of high school, he invariably has a college scholarship or an offer of a good job. He is well on his way toward becoming an ideal American citizen.

In other words, Red Henderson's plan of working with teen-agers is paying off in a fabulous and eminently satisfactory manner. "It will work in any town," Red says. "Why not try it in yours? You've nothing to lose and your gain can be truly tremendous."

Analysis

Analyze "An Ounce of Prevention." Try to learn how the author made this article of particular interest to his intended readers. Remember, at this stage you are especially interested in the *development* of the idea: What the author did with a very ordinary idea to give it appeal and genuine help to the readers of *Pen* magazine. Development is the thing to watch. Try to decide how the author used his idea to make it into the final product you have just read.

I am confident that you know not one but many sets of facts fully as worthy of presentation in an article as those which were used in "An Ounce of Prevention." Your immediate problem is to recognize your idea and develop it so it will fit the requirements of a particular periodical. To accomplish this, follow the plan that the author used in "An Ounce of Prevention." This consists of three definite steps:

1. Select an idea which can be developed into an article helpful to the readers of a given magazine.

2. Familiarize yourself with the specific needs of that magazine.

3. Develop your article so that it will actually help the readers of that magazine. (This is in the planning, not in the writing stage.)

When you have complied with these requirements, you may rest assured that you are well on the way toward producing a manuscript of which you can justly be proud, which would be welcome in the office of an editor, and would actually help the readers of his magazine. A manuscript like that is as good as money in the bank.

Chapter V

SELL YOUR ARTICLE—
THEN WRITE IT

THE QUICKEST way for you to become a selling writer is to adopt the methods of professional writers. This is not as difficult as it may appear to be. The professional writer, odd as it may seem, sells his article before he writes it. You can do the same. Your first step is to send a query letter to the editor.

WHAT IS A QUERY?

A query is a letter to an editor in which an author describes an article he wishes to write for a particular magazine. Actually, it is the most potent sales device you can use. Its purpose is to get a "go-ahead" signal from the editor which will assure you of a cordial reading for your finished article. The query saves time for you and for the editor. It enables you to write only articles for which there has been some advance interest shown by an editor. To be effective, the query letter must be skillfully written. It must dangle a choice morsel before an editor and convince him that you can write an article in a professional, generally acceptable style.

Examples

Since writing a query letter is something of an art in itself, here are a few illustrations to study:

Dear Mr. Howard:

Red Henderson, physical education instructor in Spokane, has an effective way of dealing with teen-agers. His idea is to give them favorable publicity. "If they are rewarded well for their good actions," Red reasons, "they are likely to continue in that manner."

To achieve this end, he organized the Silver Spurs, a group of high school dancers. He trained them well. They have appeared on radio, TV, toured much of the United States giving exhibition dances, and been featured in a 30-minute color film prepared by Standard Oil Company of California.

The United States Information Agency has sent their story to 77 different foreign countries. These high school boys and girls have had more favorable publicity than an average Congressman!

The article would be devoted mainly to the doings of the Silver Spurs, showing Henderson as the power behind the stage, the cause of the favorable publicity, good citizenship, and general success of the group.

Although relatively few communities might want to use Henderson's routine, perhaps thousands of communities would adopt his method. And, as a result, I am firmly convinced that we could improve the situation in regard to the teen-agers in this country today. I should like to supply this story in 1,500 words under the title "An Ounce of Prevention."

I can furnish both text and professional quality black and white photographs for illustrations. May I do this for you?

Sincerely yours,

Comment: This is a professionally written query. Its very first sentence demands reader-interest, and from there on this interest grows. There are intriguing facts in the letter which becomes more fascinating as the paragraphs unfold.

The letter is concise, the writing forceful, and the thesis —that giving children favorable publicity helps to reduce juvenile delinquency—is reasonable. An editor interested in copy for a family magazine would give such a letter careful consideration.

In fact, this is the query which resulted in the article, "An Ounce of Prevention," which appears in chapter IV of this book.

Shall we look at another example?

Dear Mr. Kartman:

You may be unaware of the fact that the world's greatest treasure hunt is going on full-blast today. I do not refer to uranium or gold mines, deposits of precious stones or fabulous treasures cached by Captain Kidd and his cohorts. Instead, I refer to bank accounts, stocks and bonds, government loans.

These are real. And the hunt is for the rightful owner— not for the cash. Its whereabouts and value are definitely established. The problem is to find the owners.

Perhaps the greatest jackpot is the United States government bonds unclaimed by their owners. It is reliably estimated that this fund alone amounts to more than $400,000,-000. If you can establish your right to any of this money, the United States Treasury will gladly give it to you—tax-free.

Finding individuals to whom unclaimed moneys belong is the work of a New York fortune hunter named Dan

Eisenberg. In this profession he has been sensationally successful.

He has salvaged for 125,000 stockholders of supposedly worthless stock a total of more than $100,000,000.

He has located more than 100 heirs of estates of $100,000 or more and 12,000 heirs to smaller sums. In all, he has produced $172,000,000 dormant dollars for wonderstruck beneficiaries.

I should like to prepare a 1,200 word story for you about Eisenberg and his work. The article—"Fabulous Forgotten Fortunes"—would include information designed to help readers who are heirs to funds they have not received.

I can supply both text and photographs for illustrations. Do you want them?

Sincerely yours,

Comment: If you were editor of a general interest publication, would you feel that here is material in which your readers would be definitely interested?

Does the letter sound convincing to you?

And, finally, does this show that the individual who wrote that letter knows how to: (1). Write in a crisp, compelling manner; (2). Keep interest rising, and (3). End the story in a satisfactory manner?

The editor of the widely distributed Sunday Supplement, *Family Weekly,* seemed to answer all of these questions in the affirmative. He asked to see the finished article, bought it, and published it.

There is no rule as to the length of a query. Generally a single page of manuscript paper is enough for such a letter. Occasionally you may want to use a second page but never more than that. Remember, you are writing a letter —not an article. So keep it short.

It follows, therefore, that you should not query an editor about an article of 500 words or less. Use the query only on full-length feature articles.

How to Write A Query

Your query is going to tell the editor a great many things about you. It will tell him whether you can start an article in an intriguing manner, whether you can keep reader interest mounting until it reaches a definite climax, whether you can write with force, and whether you know how to end an article.

This means that you must write the query in a most careful manner. Here are the specifications of a professional query:

1. Offer material in which the editor is likely to be interested.

2. Prove that you are able to write in a publishable manner. This proof will be in the composition of the letter itself. If it is intriguing, the editor will reason rightly that you can produce an article which will demand the attention of his readers.

3. Convince the editor that you have ample authoritative sources of information for the article. You will tell the editor that you have these sources—naming them, if that seems to be of particular importance.

4. Indicate the manner of organization of the article— what would come first, next, and so on. You will do this by the form of the letter, not by saying that you would begin the article with one item, follow it by another, and

end it with still something else. Your letter will be organized as the article would be.

5. Suggest a title and see that it is challenging. Titles are of tremendous importance. They show that the writer has—or does not have—a grasp of the profession.

6. End the query with a real punch. This must leave the editor entirely satisfied. And if it can cause the reader to feel that he has profited from reading the article, so much the better.

Now that you know something of a query and what it must contain, you are ready to select a magazine for which to write.

SELECTING A MAGAZINE

You have become somewhat acquainted with the small magazines. Many of them concern subjects with which you are quite familiar. If you are wise, therefore, you will select one of these publications as a possible market for an article you hope to write and sell. Let us say this is *Pen* Magazine.

You will want to learn as specifically as possible what kind of articles this periodical publishes and to understand its subject matter, style, length of articles, and the kind of illustrations it uses. To achieve this, you will study the latest market information in a writers' magazine where you may find a listing such as the following:

Pen, 444 Sherman St., Denver, Colorado. Monthly. G. Bruce Howard, editor. General and family interest articles up to 3,000 words. Original anecdotes, fillers, poems. Uses limited amount of fiction. Pays 3 cents a word and $5 for photographs on acceptance.

This is helpful. But you feel you'd like to see the publication, read some of the articles, and come to your own conclusions as to precisely what would fit into *Pen's* editorial pattern. You send twenty-five cents to the magazine and ask for the current issue. When you see it, you note that the articles deal with the family, church, school, government, community. That 3,000 word limit seems too long. Most of the *Pen* articles are much shorter than that. You conclude that, other things being equal, the 1,200 to 1,500-word piece will stand a better chance with *Pen* than the longer article.

Finally, having seen what *Pen* uses, you feel that you very well might produce an article that would appeal to its readers. You resolve to try. Now you are ready to choose a subject—a subject to fit a particular magazine.

Selecting A Subject

You begin to cast about for material for your article. The month is July. It would be several months—six or seven—before you could hope to have an article printed in *Pen*. That would mean your article might appear early next year.

Therefore, you think of material which would make a good feature at that time—in January or February—possibly an article about Lincoln or Washington.

It must be a different Lincoln or Washington story, because there will be plenty of articles in print, come February, about both of these men. Your problem is to find something that hasn't been written over and over again, something intriguing, about one or the other of these great Americans. Not too easy. But you give it thought. You do a bit of reading about Washington. In a booklet called

Historical Alexandria, Virginia you read: "Alexandria, the home town of George Washington."

This catches your eye. You read on: "Alexandria has always been known as the home of George Washington. He held the fondest hopes for its prosperity and the greatest respect for its citizens."

Here, you reason, is material which might very well make a suitable feature for *Pen*'s February issue. You decide to do a bit of preliminary research for the purpose of exploring this idea. It is necessary for you to obtain a considerable amount of information—enough to tell you without an undue amount of time and reading whether an article on this subject is actually feasible. You go on with your reading and learn many little-known but fascinating facts about Alexandria. You believe this material would make an excellent feature for the February issue of *Pen* magazine. Your next job is to make the editor agree with you, and you compose a query to the editor outlining the facts you wish to include, the plan for the article, and suggestions for its presentation. When the query letter is finished, it reads like this:

Dear Mr. Howard:

During February an all but unknown eastern seaboard city will really be in the limelight. This city—Alexandria, Virginia—contains more historic appeal than any other equal area in the United States, if not in the world. But the fact that puts it on the map in a big way this February is that it is George Washington's home town.

Next to nothing has been written on this subject. Yet here are the actual scenes of significant national events, time-scarred buildings with original furnishings, and the memorials to dauntless Colonials who gave their lives to establish the American Way of Life. For instance:

Here stands Christ Church with pew No. 60 marked by a small silver plate showing it belonged to the Washington family. Washington paid 36 pounds for it—the most paid for any pew in the church—and this was his home church. He was a vestryman in it before the Revolutionary War and a member of it when he died.

Carlyle House is here. In it George Washington was commissioned a Major in the British army. This house—it has been called the Birthplace of the Revolution and the Birthplace of the Constitution—is regarded as the most historical residence in America. Its story is fascinating.

Here stands Gadsby's Tavern which George Washington occupied while recruiting his Rangers in 1754. In this building patriots staged the first celebration of the adoption of the Federal Constitution. Standing on the steps of this old building, Washington delivered his farewell address to his Alexandria friends before going to New York to assume his duties as First President of the United States.

The world-famous Masonic temple, which was erected in honor of George Washington, too, stands here, a museum filled with hundreds of items concerning Washington.

These are but a few of the facets of George Washington's home town. I feel that a thousand words and several photographs would make a picture story suitable for the February issue of *Pen* magazine.

I can give you a professional feature—both text and photographs. If you would like it, I could give an excellent transparency of Christ Church—a 4x5 in rich color—for your cover. It would make a really outstanding cover. Or, I could give you the same thing in black and white.

Does this idea appeal to you for an article in *Pen*?

Sincerely yours,

Editor's Analysis

Let us examine this query as if we were the editor to whom it was sent. We should remember that this is all he has to help him decide whether or not to encourage the writer to complete the article. In this letter we find the following significant facts:

1. The letter deals with timely material. It contains new information—facts which the reader very likely does not know and in which he would be interested. As such, it is subject matter worth publishing.

2. The letter, although short, tells the complete story. It would appear that the writer, therefore, understands what should go into an article and has the ability to compress his material.

3. The first sentence of the letter arouses interest. It lures the reader on, makes him want to know why this all but unknown eastern seaboard city will be in the limelight. This indicates that the writer understands how to present material in an intriguing fashion.

4. As the letter progresses, our interest rises. This would suggest that the writer knows how to organize his facts.

5. Since the letter ends on a satisfactory note, it would appear that the writer has carefully chosen the material to be included in the article, bearing in mind the final effect the article should have on the reader.

6. There isn't a single false note in the entire letter. This cannot be accidental; it means that the person who wrote the letter is working in a medium in which he is entirely at home. In all probability he could write an article in a thoroughly professional manner.

Editorial Decision

The editor is ready to decide whether he will encourage the writer to submit the article for consideration. In all likelihood, if he has an opening for such an article, he will indicate to the writer that he will be glad to consider the finished article.

Here is the letter I received in response to the foregoing query:

Dear Mr. Henry:

I am sure you'll be glad to know that we are interested in seeing the article you mentioned.

I believe it can be covered in around 1,000 words and if we can use five or six photos, it should make an excellent photo story.

If you'll send all illustrations in 8x10 glossies, we will be able to take care of it if we decide to use one for the cover. So there will be no future misunderstanding, Mr. Henry, I want to mention this request is made on a purely speculative basis, and we may or may not find the article acceptable.

Cordially yours,
GLENN A. REINEKE

This is the type of letter most editors of small magazines use in replying to queries. Translated into plain English, it says: "If your article is as good as your letter, I'll buy it."

When you get such a letter, your next step is to reply to the editor. Here is the reply which I sent in response to the foregoing communication:

Dear Mr. Reineke:

Thanks for your letter of August 15. I am glad that you are interested in the story of George Washington's home town. I shall try to give you a first-class article and suitable photographs for illustrations. These will reach you within the next two weeks.

Sincerely yours,

Final Test

Now it was up to me to produce an article which would fulfill the promises in my letter. I completed my research, drafted the article, typed it on good bond, and obtained the necessary photographs. Then I wrote:

Dear Mr. Reineke:

Herewith is the George Washington's Home Town piece regarding which we have corresponded. Too, I am enclosing a number of black and white photographs for possible use as illustrations.

Sincerely yours,

And with this letter I submitted the following manuscript:

GEORGE WASHINGTON'S HOME TOWN *

By Omer Henry

During February an all but unknown eastern seaboard city —Alexandria, Virginia—will be in the limelight since Alexandria is the home town of George Washington.

Here also were the scenes of many significant national events; time-scarred buildings with their original furnishings,

* Reprinted by permission of *Pen Magazine*.

memorials to dauntless Colonials who gave their lives to establish the American Way of Life.

What, specifically, is here that harkens back to the days of George Washington? A thousand things. For instance:

Norford Inn, a picturesque hostelry with an old-world atmosphere, has been in continuous operation since 1815. It was a regular port of call for horse-drawn stagecoaches of Colonial Days and housed overnight such celebrities as Daniel Webster, John Calhoun, and George Washington. It still retains an air of the former days.

At the opposite side of the city stands Friendship Firehouse, home of the Fire Company which Washington organized. In 1775 he presented the Company with a fire engine which he had bought from a French company. The Friendship Fire Company still functions as an historical organization and the Washington fire engine, hand propelled and operated, is on display at the Firehouse.

Too, here you may see the first free school of Northern Virginia which Washington established and supported.

It is small wonder that these features, much as they were in Washington's day, give Alexandria a genuine flavor of the past.

A short distance from the first free school stands the Stabler-Leadbeater Apothecary Shop, the oldest in Virginia and second oldest in continual operation in America. Now conducted as a museum, it will amaze you with its stock of ancient wares judged to be the most complete in America.

There hundreds of bottles of many sizes and colors, mortars and pestles of many shapes and sizes, old eyeglasses, weights, scales, and everything the early American bought at his apothecary shop may be seen along with extraordinary documents such as this:

"Mrs. Washington desires Mr. Stabler will send by the bearer a quart bottle of his best castor oil and the bill for it."

Within easy walking distance of the Old Apothecary Shop stands impressive Christ Church (Episcopal). George Washington not only was a vestryman when the church was planned but he purchased pew No. 60 for 36 pounds, the highest price paid for any pew, and remained a member throughout his life.

In the very shadow of Christ Church one Sunday morning in 1774, surrounded by the congregation, every one of whom he knew well, Washington advocated withdrawing allegiance from King George and declared he would fight to uphold the independence of the Colonies.

Nine years later, after the war, he returned to Mount Vernon on Christmas Eve. The next day found him back in his accustomed seat in Christ Church to hear the Reverend Griffith proclaim that peace and good will reigned once more in the land. No one bowed his head more deeply than the great general.

With the establishment of American independence the church tax disappeared. This necessitated a new method of raising funds. Accordingly, on April 25, 1785, George Washington and other prominent laymen of this Parish met in Alexandria and signed a contract binding themselves, their heirs, executors, and assigns to pay annually to the Minister and Vestry the sum of five pounds for each pew assigned to them.

The church treasures today Washington's Bible which was presented by his grandson after the general's death.

Hundreds of famous people, including Marshal Foch, David Lloyd George, Winston Churchill, and United States Presidents Wilson, Roosevelt, Truman, and Eisenhower, have worshipped in Christ Church. It may well be regarded as one of the most historic churches in the entire United States.

An even more famous Alexandria feature is Gadsby's Tavern. The building itself, regarded as one of the best remaining examples of Georgian architecture, is especially noted for its fine handcarved woodwork. Architects planning the period rooms recently installed in the Smithsonian Institution, studied Gadsby's for authentic guidance.

George Washington used this building as his Headquarters when recruiting Rangers for his French and Indian War campaign. In it Colonial patriots staged the first celebration of the adoption of the Federal Constitution. And, prior to going to New York to be installed as first President of the United States, Washington stood on the steps of this old building and made his farewell address.

In February, 1799, Washington attended an elegant Ball given at Gadsby's Tavern in celebration of his birthday which, as it happened, proved to be his last.

Even today, as in Washington's time, Gadsby's Tavern is a playhouse. And in keeping with tradition it presents old plays. The 1958 offering was *She Stoops to Conquer,* the Oliver Goldsmith drama, written almost two centuries ago.

The producers, with authentically costumed actors, white-bonneted and aproned maids to act as ushers, a major domo to announce your name as you entered the theater, and a bevy of hostesses decked out in finery which would have made Nellie Custis green with envy, created a play such as Washington enjoyed.

At intermission you were invited to suck oranges through peppermint sticks or sip Colonial punch or coffee.

This ancient red brick building, a social and cultural center for more than two centuries, is one of the most historic landmarks in the "Old Dominion," the Union's most historic state.

Undoubtedly Alexandria's most fascinating building is Carlyle House. In 1752 John Carlyle, a Scotch merchant and ship owner, built this enormous frame residence near the waterfront.

The stone foundation for this famous home originally was a fort built in the early days of American colonization, probably about 1640, as a refuge from the Indians. In addition it included two stone dungeons, into which you may walk today, where the Colonists held Indian prisoners. Because of the great number of executions which occurred here, the fort became known as the Hanging Fort.

It was in this house that George Washington began his military career as a Major in the British Army under General Edward Braddock during the French and Indian War.

Since Carlyle House was Braddock's Headquarters, he conducted various conferences in it. At one of these, he and five Colonial governors—Dinwiddie of Virginia, Shirley of Massachusetts, De Lancey of New York, Sharp of Maryland, and Morris of Pennsylvania—discussed plans for waging and financing the French and Indian War. These men decided to impose a Stamp Act upon the Colonists.

Some years later the Act became a reality. And, inasmuch as that Act became a prime cause of the struggle for independence, Carlyle House has been called the Birthplace of the Revolutionary War.

Following the enforcement of the Stamp Act, Colonial statesmen held numerous conferences at Carlyle House, protesting the Act and looking forward to freedom from the Mother country. Later, delegates from Alexandria participated in the Philadelphia convention which framed the Constitution of the United States. Therefore, Carlyle House has a legitimate right to its proudest title—Birthplace of the Constitution.

In light of these facts it is understandable that this ancient and colorful residence is considered to be one of the most historic homes in America.

Truly Alexandria offers a quality that has all but vanished, a genuine Colonial atmosphere based not on reconstructed buildings and scenes but on originals. Here is history—colorful, inspiring, and intensely moving American history in the raw, a significant aspect of our priceless heritage.

The fact that Alexandria has maintained this atmosphere

is heartening. It clearly demonstrates that she is proud of her most illustrious citizen, hero of Valley Forge, Trenton, and Yorktown. "He," all of Alexandria seems to say, "was not only first in peace and war but also first in the hearts of his countrymen—even in his own home town!"

Editorial Response

It was only a few days after I mailed this manuscript that *Pen* sent me a check for the article. It appeared in the February 1959 issue under the title *Washington's Town*, and it indicates that my query made the sale. It convinced the editor that here was suitable material for his magazine and that I could present it in an acceptable manner.

This is the way a professional writer works. And if you follow the foregoing blueprint, you, too, can sell your articles before you write them.

Chapter VI

RESEARCH

••

ONE OF your most valuable assets as a writer is your ability to do research well. It is through your reading, questioning of others, and general observation—research in one form or another—that you obtain information which is worth reporting and publishing. Your astuteness in this respect may very well be the keystone to your success as a writer.

This means that although the idea of your article is good, that is only half of the battle. Far less than half, to be entirely truthful, for what you do with the idea is far more important than the idea itself. An ordinary writer with a perfectly wonderful idea may produce a worthless article, yet a skilled writer with a commonplace idea may transform it into an unforgettable bit of prose.

What is the difference? In many instances, it is a matter of research. Therefore, it is essential that you learn well some basic facts about research.

LIBRARIES AND READING

You will find the library is your greatest source of information. Even though you may be well educated, you may not be fully aware of the vast amount of information available in even a small library.

Scholars who have devoted the major portions of their lives to research have produced literally hundreds of reference books of particular value to you as a writer. Among these are the *Reader's Guide to Periodical Literature*, various indexes to specialized publications, and, in the newspaper field, the New York *Times Index*.

In using the library, you must consider publication dates. Just because information is new to you is no proof that it is up-to-date. You must make sure that the facts which you give in an article are currently accepted as true by the authorities in that field, not merely facts which were regarded as true a quarter of a century ago but have subsequently been thoroughly discredited.

Become well acquainted with your library. In the "vertical files" you will find pamphlets, brochures, and unbound material which may supply the very information you need for a particular article. Also, many libraries maintain files of newspaper and magazine clippings on particular subjects. When you face a research problem, you should immediately solicit your librarian's assistance.

Since much of your information comes from the written word, you need to understand the copyright law. Basically, it is designed to protect the author. It forbids a writer to copy the work of another so long as the copyright is in effect.

The first term of copyright in the United States is 28 years, and a copyright may be renewed for an equal period of time. Any work published more than 56 years, however, is in the public domain—which means that it is no longer protected by copyright—insofar as the original version is concerned.

You must understand, however, that an idea cannot be

copyrighted. Once an author has published information, that data is in the public domain; it is entirely ethical and legal for you to utilize such material in your research. However, you must not copy it—with or without quotation marks—or any part of it except with the written consent of the copyright owner.

As a researcher, you will need to form new reading habits. This is necessary because you are searching for information, not merely perusing a book, story, or article. If you attempt to use the same reading habits in research which you utilize for general reading, you will never finish a research project.

An expert researcher will be able to tell in a matter of minutes whether a book contains information pertinent to the article he is doing. The table of contents and index are useful aids in this respect, but even when you find data that is of value to you, read it rapidly. Learn to grasp the essence of a paragraph or a page in the quickest time possible.

NOTE-TAKING

Whether you are making notes from published materials or as a result of an interview or observation, you must be accurate and complete and you should mark each note to enable you to find its source again quickly.

I find it advantageous to record notes on 3"x5" pieces of white bond paper (or index cards), placing but one anecdote, fact, or observation on each piece of paper, thus:

During the American Revolutionary war, American sharp-shooters using long rifles were able to hit a target 8"x10" at a distance of ¼ mile. These men picked off the British officers with such regularity that the British became most angry and called the Americans murderers.

X-14

The symbol X-14 refers to a particular document in my file, thus enabling me readily to find the source of this information if it is necessary that I do so. If you take notes in this fashion, you can sort them into appropriate groups to facilitate your composition when you begin drafting the article.

Not long ago a professional journal for writers carried a statement to the effect that the researcher should obtain ten times the amount of information he wished to use in his article. I disagree completely. Why should one obtain data he cannot use? The writer's business is to complete articles for publication with all the efficiency possible. One does that by going directly to the point in his research.

In order to do this easily, you must first know what you intend to say in your article—its theme. When you have decided on this, you can judge what material you will need to support that theme.

Secondly, you must understand that the purpose of research is to gather local color, facts, and incidents which you can use in your article. Disregard all other information you may find in your research. Keep directly to the point of your article. It is your job as a researcher to obtain material that will help you to build a compelling article, not necessarily a long one.

New Sources of Information

Always be on the alert for new sources of information. There are thousands of them: industrial concerns, celebrities with press agents, politicians seeking to build up a following, government offices, organizations of every kind, churches.

Not long ago I wanted to do an article about the Iwo Jima Memorial in Washington, D.C. I asked the United States Marine Corps Information Office for background material and photographs. The Marines sent me such a file of data that I needed to do very little outside research to complete the article.

The Government Printing Office publishes thousands of booklets on almost every conceivable subject. These pamphlets, although often written in a colorless style, are generally well researched and so are valuable as source material for the writer.

Experts in a given field are generally glad to cooperate with serious writers who show that they have an understanding of the subject.

INTERVIEWS

One important means of obtaining information for your articles is by interviewing. A considerable part of your work as a writer of non-fiction will consist of talking with all types of people, attempting to elicit from them facts which you desire. Therefore, the following suggestions may be of help to you in this respect:

1. Plan each interview carefully before you begin it. Try to know precisely what you hope to obtain from the interviewee. Learn enough about the subject which you propose to discuss to enable you to talk intelligently about it.

2. Observe the interviewee, his appearance, age, mannerisms, and mode of speaking. If you are in his home, office, or place of business, make careful note of the surroundings.

You may find these of value to you in the article you are doing.

3. Seek specific information, not generalities, about the person you are interviewing. Obtain as many pertinent anecdotes as possible. One obstacle you will meet is the interviewee's inability to recall incidents you would like to use. There is but one answer to this problem—persistence.

4. Be methodical about an interview. For instance, if you are attempting to learn about a business, you may want to use a set of questions such as these:

a. By whom, when, and under what circumstances was the shop founded?

b. What categories and price ranges of merchandise do you carry?

c. What does the shop or office look like? What is its size? Any available photographs of it? Clippings?

d. Do you offer the customer any special services?

e. Is there anything about the store that gives it a personality of its own?

f. What is your approach to advertising and sales promotion? Some examples would be helpful.

g. What, in your opinion, is the greatest problem facing the independent retailer today?

h. Any other pertinent information that you care to add will be welcome.

5. Make sure that the story is true before you publish it. Sometimes the temptation is strong to rush ahead with information that fits perfectly into your article. For instance, when I was doing an article about the Washington taxi company, one of the drivers told me a fabulous story

about the Vice-President of the United States. My immediate reaction was to use it in the article. It was a perfect anecdote—perfect with one highly important qualification —I could not publish it unless I knew it was entirely true and that the Vice-President did not object to the publication of this incident. There was but one way to establish the facts beyond all possible doubt—get in touch with the Vice-President himself. I put the anecdote into the article, sent it to the Vice-President, and asked if it were true and whether he objected to its publication. He replied at once that the story was true and that he had no objection to its publication. That made the article perfect.

BUILD YOUR OWN FILES

One of the most valuable bits of information I can pass on to you about research is also one of the easiest to utilize. It concerns your filing system. This need not be elaborate or complex.

Start with a number—say a dozen—Manila folders. Tab each one with a subject which you may wish to use in an article, or in articles. The headings might be: Washington Monument, Abraham Lincoln, Sex, Religion, Safety, Health, Vacation. When you find in a newspaper or magazine something which you feel might be helpful to you in researching an article on one of these subjects, clip that article and put it into the proper folder.

You will be surprised at how rapidly these folders expand, and when you get ready to write an article on one of these subjects, you will have in your own files considerable up-to-the-minute information—data which otherwise might cost you much in time and effort.

Also, when you research an article, keep your notes. It is

foolish for you to discard your notes simply because you have sold one article on a given subject. Slant the material differently and do an article for another magazine. The original notes may be sufficient for two or three articles.

THEORY IN PRACTICE

So much for theory in researching. Now, to show you as specifically as possible how to handle this tremendously important aspect of writing, let us consider an actual example. We shall follow it step by step from idea, through planning, researching, and even the writing. It all began, of course, with the idea.

Idea

Some time ago I learned that many men and boys were manufacturing rifles in basement workshops. This appeared to me to be a subject for an article in one of the small magazines for men.

Planning

I began to think about what such an article should say —what message it should carry. This was the beginning of the planning of the article. Before I could answer this question, it was necessary that I do some preliminary research. That gave me amazing information. Literally thousands of men and boys—even women—were building bench rest rifles by hand. Furthermore, these guns were remarkably accurate. I decided to build an article about these rifles— an article which would tell of their spectacular accuracy.

My next step was to get a "go-ahead" for the article. In response to my query, the editor of *Woodmen of the World* said he would like to see the article. With a magazine interested in the story, I set about doing the necessary research.

Researching

Although I knew a bit about rifles, I was completely uninformed on the subject of manufacturing them. Neither had I any considerable knowledge about making ammunition. So it was necessary for me to acquire quite a fund of information on these subjects before I attempted to write the article.

First, I considered possible sources. My article, I hoped, would be authoritative. Therefore I must obtain data from men who knew most on this subject, from books which were prepared by individuals recognized as experts. A bit of research told me that Colonel Townsend Whelen, famous hunter, shooter, and author, is one of the country's best informed men about bench rest rifles.

The card index at the library told me that Colonel Whelen had recently edited a volume entitled *The Ultimate in Rifle Precision,* Handbook of the National Bench Rest Shooters Association. This, clearly, was the place for me to begin my serious research.

I obtained this book. In it I found the history of bench rest shooting, the rules and regulations of the National Bench Rest Shooters Association, how to measure targets. Here, too, were chapters dealing with barrel making, stock bedding, bullet making, and the telescopic sight. Here, indeed, was a wealth of thoroughly authoritative information. I made notes of such facts as I felt would be useful to me in the preparation of this article.

Next I went to the National Rifle Association and asked for information. There I learned that *The National Rifle-*

man had carried two articles on this subject. I studied these, all the time aware that what I intended to show in my own article was that the modern bench rest rifle is superlatively accurate.

I talked with bench rest rifle experts at the National Rifle Association and reviewed certain publications on file in that office.

By the time I went to the local library to find recently published material on the subject, I was beginning to feel that I had a smattering of knowledge on this fascinating subject.

At the library I found a number of articles had appeared recently, each one dealing with some phase of bench rest shooting. I made proper notes. Then I felt I was ready to begin interviewing men who made and used these rifles.

My first interviewee was Dr. Donald E. Callar, a dentist, who is an outstanding bench rest rifle expert. I talked with him in his workshop, noted his gun collection, watched him make ammunition by hand.

"The man," he told me, "who uses commercial ammunition at a bench rest meet might just as well stay at home.

"In order to learn the best possible combination of powder and bullet, shape, weight, and construction of bullet, and kind of powder, bench rest shooters have done considerable scientific experimentation."

I watched Dr. Callar putting cartridges together. For a .219 Donaldson Wasp, he weighed powder as carefully as a master pharmacist compounding a potent prescription. With a "dripper" that would add a single particle of powder at a time to the scales pan, he measured out the exact charge necessary to produce the greatest possible accuracy under a set of fixed conditions.

The precision with which Callar worked amazed me. But he took it all for granted. "Amateur gunsmiths in basement workshops," he said, "are producing more accurate rifles than the top manufacturers in million-dollar factories. These unknown devotees to the art of precision shooting are even excelling H. M. Pope, the Stradivarius of rifledom."

Next I attended a bench rest meet where a couple of hundred men, boys, and women—all bench rest enthusiasts—in colorful attire and with precision-made rifles and meticulously manufactured ammunition met to test their guns and ammunition.

Armed with camera and notebook, I spent most of a day at this meet, saw the shooters in action, examined their rifles, the bench rests from which they fired, the targets, noted them being measured. I talked with dozens of these men, boys, and women. When I left the match, I felt that I was entirely prepared to do an article on the subject.

At my desk again, I found a stack of perhaps two hundred 3″x5″ bits of paper, each one containing a notation such as these:

. . . There is no question but what a free floating barrel gives better results than one which is not free floating.

. . . Rifle barrels as turned out by several of today's top makers are the most accurate barrels ever made.

. . . We are prone to think of a rifle barrel as being rigid. Actually a sporter weight barrel flaps up and down like a shirttail in a breeze when a bullet goes through it.

I cite these points merely to show that it was necessary for me to learn a thousand details about bench rest shooting before I could hope to produce an authoritative article on the subject. I learned these details through research—reading, interviewing, and observing men and women at a bench rest rifle match.

With all of this done and properly noted, I was ready to tackle the toughest of all writing jobs—organizing the material, mixing it with a judicious amount of imagination, making it readable yet true—and putting it into manuscript form. I hammered out the article, and here is the manuscript I offered to the editor:

WORLD'S BEST MARKSMEN *

Compared with today's bench rest riflemen, Annie Oakley, Buffalo Bill, and Daniel Boone—all renowned for their shooting skill—were rank amateurs. Not one of them would get even to the semi-finals in a modern bench rest match.

What is bench rest shooting?

It is a manner of shooting which practically eliminates the human error of marksmanship, thus permitting the shortcomings and peculiarities of rifle and ammunition to stand alone.

"Almost anyone," says Donald E. Callar, expert bench rest marksman, "can outshoot his rifle. Therefore, precision firearms are all-important to the serious rifleman."

To document his claim, he points to the records of the bench rest shooters. Many of them, as he says, are placing ten consecutive bullets in a dime-sized circle from a distance of 200 yards. Others are doing even better.

In an official meet in 1955, George Herman of Omaha, firing 10 shots at each of five targets from a distance of 200 yards, scored .4100″. That is, the average distance from center to center of the bullets farthest apart in each group of 10 shots

* Reprinted with permission of *Woodmen of the World*.

was 4100/10,000th of an inch—considerable less than the diameter of a dime.

Clair Taylor of Pennsylvania, firing 5 five-shot groups from a distance of 200 yards, scored .3032".

The record of Paul Dinant of San Diego, California, is even more startling. From 100 yards he fired 5 shots for a score of .1057". In other words, it was approximately 1/10 of an inch from center to center of the two bullets farthest apart in his group of shots.

That is, for all practical purposes, Dinant put 5 consecutive slugs through one bullet hole from a distance of 100 yards.

Billy the Kid and all his cohorts of gunslinging immortals never scored anything even remotely like that.

Shooters News, official publication of the National Bench Rest Shooters Association, reports that a majority of the competitive bench rest shooters attain an average for 10-shot groups of less than a minute angle—approximately 1" per hundred yards—of accuracy and that the best shooters with the best rifles consistently score much higher than that.

Bench rests, superior rifles, and superlative ammunition enable these modern marksmen to perform in such an amazing manner.

A bench rest is a device—quite often a wooden table—designed to hold a rifle steady. It is not a machine bench, and it does not lock a rifle in position. It permits a rifle to jump, vibrate, and recoil in a normal manner, and it is readily adaptable to any rifle.

According to the regulation of the National Bench Rest Shooters Association, it must be so constructed as to permit the shooter to fire the gun by contracting the trigger with his finger.

Although these benches are interesting, the firearms utilized in the meets are utterly fascinating. They range from the old-time muzzle loader to the sleek customized gun which may sell for as much as a thousand dollars and is worth every cent of it.

All bench rest rifles, whether breech or muzzle loaders, to be eligible for use in an official bench rest match, must fall into one or the other of the following types:

Varmint Class. There is no restriction on caliber or scope power of rifles used in this class, but the combined weight of the rifle and scope must not exceed 13 pounds. The maximum diameter of the barrel breech of a custom-built gun, to be eligible for competition in this class, is 1.250″; that of the muzzle .900″.

Open Class. Any rifle, with any safe ammunition, any sights, and any weight may be used if its detonation is actuated by the finger.

These specifications permit the use of the famous Kentucky long rifle in bench rest shooting matches, and many riflemen utilize these slim, elegant guns which helped to win two wars and open the West.

Some of the guns are gigantic. For instance: Richard K. James, Washington, D.C., owns a muzzle loader which weighs 38 pounds, has a 42″ barrel which is 1⅝″ in diameter at the muzzle, and shoots a .50 caliber bullet.

Guns like this often make remarkable records. Walter Grote, of Canton, Ohio, using a huge 1880 rifle in a bench rest match at Camp Perry, recently shot perfect bull's eye scores at 100, 200, 300, and even 600 yards.

Where does one get a bench rest firearm?

Some of them are available through dealers but a far more fertile source—particularly of customized guns—is the band of skilled amateur and professional rifle makers who, through bench rest shooting tests, have developed weapons which closely approach the ultimate in precision.

Donald E. Callar, mentioned earlier in this article, falls into that category. For several years he has been experimenting with rifles and has produced some excellent guns.

Using both guns and ammunition which he has manufactured, in national competitions with famed marksmen, he often carries away a considerable portion of the prize money. Therefore, his ideas about rifle making should be worth while. Here is how he goes about the job:

"The barrel of a rifle," he says, "is the very soul of the gun. Barrels by American specialists have always led the world in accuracy and they are better today than ever before. Even so, in constructing a rifle, I carefully select only the best barrel blanks from the most noted manufacturers."

Although the manufacturer does the rifling, there remains plenty for the rifle builder to do in connection with the barrel. One of his first actions is to cut it to the proper length.

There is a general opinion that the long-barreled rifle is more accurate than the short-barreled weapon. As a result, some guns—particularly the muzzle loaders—have extremely long barrels.

"The length of the barrel," Callar says, "is no gauge of the rifle's accuracy. No barrel need be more than 30″ long to insure its best accuracy. A longer barrel may be an actual handicap because a muzzle-heavy rifle won't balance properly on the sandbags on the bench rest."

Other experts agree with Callar. "I personally prefer a 24″ barrel," says G. R. Douglas, one of the most successful modern barrel makers. "Actually a 24″ barrel is just as accurate as one 30″ long, although it may not have enough weight to absorb recoil or to balance as well."

A mighty lathe in Callar's workshop does much toward fashioning a prize-winning barrel for one of his customized rifles. Because of the hardness of the steel in it, the "turning off" of a barrel is slow work, the chambering even more difficult.

"An error of a few thousandths of an inch in this phase of the job," Callar says, "would not only ruin my chance for winning any match in which I used the imperfect barrel but would blast sky high my reputation as a craftsman."

Callar's rifle barrels are free-floating. That is, one may place a piece of paper between the stock and the barrel at all points but one. This feature, by eliminating the stock interference to barrel vibrations—a barrel flaps up and down like a shirt-tail in a breeze when a bullet goes through it—improves the gun's accuracy.

Realizing the importance of a proper stock, Callar works as painstakingly with this aspect of the rifle as with any other. "The stock of a bench rest rifle," he says, "should be heavy and thick. The forearm should be heavy and more or less a 'beavertail' shape and should not be longer than half of the length of the barrel."

The wood used in a stock should be well-seasoned and treated inside and out with a filler and oil. A laminated stock is often a help but it is not a necessity. Weight gives stiffness and lamination minimizes warping, shrinking, and expansion.

Callar designs the stock to suit the particular barrel he plans to use in a given rifle, then cuts it from solid walnut and mortises the slots and grooves in it to the thousandth of an inch for precision bedding of the barrel and action.

When all of this is done and the stock is perfectly fitted to the barrel, Callar hand-carves the pistol grip in a 60-degree diamond pattern. In finishing the stock, he sands it down, fills and polishes with linseed oil, and then rubs the stock to a mirror gloss.

So far as actions—the firing mechanism—of a rifle are concerned, Callar utilizes the German Mauser to a considerable extent. Because he adjusts the trigger mechanism so delicately, he describes his guns as "hair-triggered." It requires only a "butterfly touch" to discharge one of these rifles. This means

greater accuracy for, by making the trigger pull extremely
light, Callar insures the marksman that he will not pull off
the target in firing the gun.

The real problem today, according to Callar, is that of optics.
"One can shoot," he says, "only as well as he can see."

In order to make his product as nearly perfect as possible,
Callar installs a 30-power scope on each rifle.

"But," says Callar, "if one is to be a serious rival in today's
bench rest shooting meets, he needs more than an excellent
rifle. His ammunition must be superb."

Bench rest shooters have done considerable scientific experimentation with various types of cartridges. "Generally
speaking," says Colonel Townsend Whelen, one of the nation's
outstanding authorities, "we have found that the most accurate cartridges at 100 and 200 yards are the .222 Remington,
the .219 Donaldson Wasp, and the .22/250 Varminter, and
slight modifications of them."

A high percentage of bench rest shooters customize their
own ammunition. This is a difficult and dangerous undertaking. To determine exactly the right charge for a bullet of
given size and weight in a specified gun over a stipulated range
is a rather complicated matter. A too-heavy charge may prove
disastrous. Therefore, amateurs should attempt loading ammunition only under the supervision of one experienced in
the art.

"I weigh the powder which goes into a cartridge," Callar
says, "as carefully as a pharmacist compounds a prescription.
I have a 'dripper' which enables me to add a single particle
of powder to the scales pan in order that I may have the
precise charge necessary to produce the greatest possible accuracy under a set of fixed conditions."

The bullets, too, are customized. "For the Donaldson Wasp,"
Callar says, "I use exactly 55 grains of lead wire. I note a
definite difference in the quality of the ammunition if I vary

the weight of the bullet or the amount of the charge by even a few grains."

And so it is from one end of the country to the other. Thousands of skilled amateur and professional gun and ammunition makers have practically eliminated the human error from bench rest shooting.

How much closer the bench rest shooters may approach the ultimate in accuracy remains to be seen, but no weapon has even approached the precision of the modern bench rest rifle. And the bench rest shooter is, beyond all doubt, the world's top-flight marksman.

Only a few days after I mailed this manuscript, I had a letter from the editor. He liked the story, enclosed a check for it, and said that he planned to publish it soon. I breathed a sigh of relief. The article had sold. My research had been successful.

This same type of research will be of material aid to you in producing articles for magazines. The fundamental basis for worthwhile articles is competent research. See that you use it in every article you write. It can become your private gold mine.

Chapter VII

HOW TO ORGANIZE YOUR ARTICLE

••

THE FACT that you choose suitable subject matter and research it well is no proof that you will sell your articles. Important as these elements are, there is another far more necessary than either. If you fail to understand this ingredient, you may as well save your postage.

What is this ingredient? *Organization.* Unless you build your article properly, the editor is likely to return it with the comment that it doesn't "come off." This expression merely means that the article fails to satisfy the editor. And one of the major reasons why an article fails to satisfy an editor—or any other discerning reader—is that it isn't properly organized.

If you hope to sell articles with any degree of regularity, you must learn how to put them together in a forceful manner. You must see that they, when finished, have real impact. Here are some suggestions—article blueprints, explanations and examples of article architecture—designed to aid you in this exacting aspect of the profession.

CHRONOLOGICAL APPROACH

Perhaps the easiest method of organizing an article is by the straight chronological method. Using this plan, you report events in time order. But if you are a careful craftsman, you also give attention to other factors. For instance:

a) You will select as the opening of the article a bit of information or an incident which fulfills the time requirement and also demands attention.

b) More, it is not enough to report the remainder of your article chronologically. There is the matter of reader interest to consider. Therefore, you should arrange your material in order of ascending interest.

c) Even though you use this approach, you must see that the most exciting event you have to report happens at the end of the article. Otherwise, you will produce an anticlimax.

Also, in considering the arrangement of the various parts of your article, you should consider the wordage required for each incident. Since the less important facets of the story will be reported briefly, you may find it advisable to place them in the first part of the article. The longer, more forceful units will appear later in the article, nearer the climax.

It is clear, therefore, that time is but one of the elements you must consider in organizing your article according to the straight chronological method. In some articles, this method of organizing an article is ideal. For instance:

ADVENTURES IN COOKING OUT *

By Beverly Ginsberg

Our next-door neighbors recently built an attractive patio and furnished it with gay, comfortable lounges. That was bad enough. But the trouble really started when, with seemingly

* Reprinted by permission of the author, Beverly Ginsberg, from *Minutes* (August, 1959).

no effort, they became versatile experts at cooking outdoors on a charcoal brazier.

A couple of good whiffs of their meat sizzling over an open grill and we were hooked. A sample taste of their juicy barbe-cued ribs convinced my husband that we too must try our hand at charcoaling.

Now, eight raw T-bone steaks and countless burned ham-burgers later, I have come to the conclusion that barbecuing is an art and we're not artists.

Not that we haven't invested in the proper equipment. We bought everything from the brazier and motorized spit to an electric fire starter. (What respectable master chef can light a fire with an ordinary liquid starter?) Then there were the incidentals, like a picnic table and plastic dishes, a fire rake, tongs, shovel, mitts, apron, and cap. These took a sizable bite out of our vacation fund, but who wants to travel when he can stay home and enjoy food fit for the gods?

The instruction book said, on page seven, "Spit barbecuing is probably the easiest form." Our course was as clear-cut as an airman's on automatic pilot. For our first cook-out, we would roast chickens on the motorized spit.

The brazier was all set up before we remembered we had neither an outdoor electrical outlet nor an extension cord. The neighbors loaned us a cord, which was the least they could do after roasting Cornish hens right under our noses that afternoon.

Following directions, we placed the chickens on the spit rod, but we had no twine for tying. This might explain why the birds immediately fell off the rod into the coals.

We'd just replaced them when it started to rain, so we moved operations to the front porch. Before long we'd not only filled the house with flavor-laden smoke but charred the chicken and fried the electric cord.

The peanut butter sandwiches tasted pretty good.

Upon advice of our neighbors, we next tried kabobs. At least we didn't drop them into the fire. They fell off the skewers onto the ground. I served peanut butter sandwiches again.

"We'll try something simpler," my determined husband said flatly. "We can't possibly ruin hot dogs and corn on the cob."

He's not only an optimist, but rarely wrong. That's why it's hard to understand why the wieners were crisp and the corn hard and blackened. I wondered about it the whole time I was preparing the peanut butter sandwiches.

We kept trying. My husband thought there must be something wrong with the fires he built, so he practiced one whole afternoon. Results: three pounds of cremated hamburger for the dog and one scorched garage.

I tried, too. Our house isn't built like those pictured in magazines, with doors conveniently opening out onto a patio, so every afternoon I'd haul food and dishes half way through the house, out the side door, and around to the back. How would a psychiatrist explain why I always forgot at least one item each meal?

Then there were the children—Theirs and Ours. As we settled down for a meal at the picnic table, at least half the neighborhood moppets would gather by our terrace, weak from hunger. Obviously their parents hadn't fed them for at least an hour. While they watched, wide-eyed, our kiddies jiggled impatiently at the table. It seems that our meals always interrupted more important things like bike races, digging holes to China, or lemonade stands.

Last week end, we definitely decided to give up outdoor cooking and return to the conveniences of our pleasant little kitchen. As I write this, though, I can smell the neighbors' steaks and I am almost convinced we should give barbecuing one more try.

But, first, have we any peanut butter?

Article Blueprint

What can you learn from this short article?

If you study it methodically, you can learn much that will help you to produce better planned articles of your own. You may begin this study with the realization that an article—precisely as a building—is made up of smaller units. These smaller units in an article are facts, observations, and anecdotes.

Before the author managed to put all of these together into a publishable bit of prose, she had to arrange them in a suitable manner. Most authors do this by preparing an outline which becomes the structural framework of the article. When we reduce "Adventures in Cooking Out" to the framework, or outline, it looks like this:

I. Adventures in cooking out
   A. Neighbors build patio
   B. Neighbors start outdoor cooking
   C. Author's family decides to try outdoor cooking
   D. Results
   E. Purchasing equipment
   F. Electric cord missing
   G. Attempt to barbecue chicken
   H. Results
   I. Rain
   J. Set up brazier on front porch
   K. Results
   L. Peanut butter sandwiches
   M. Tried kabobs
   N. Results
   O. Hot dogs and corn on cob

    P. Results
    Q. Peanut butter sandwiches
    R. Cremated hamburger
    S. Author tries her hand
    T. Results
    U. Dinner at last
    V. Decided to give up outdoor cooking
    W. The lure of neighbor's sizzling steaks
    X. Do we have peanut butter?

It may surprise you to learn that in so short an article there are so many separate units. Note the arrangement of these various bits of architecture in this article. The cause-effect relationship which you see repeated over and over again is a device to follow in your article writing. This will add credibility to your article.

By understanding the structural framework of published articles, you will be better prepared to plan an article of your own. All you need do is to outline it. When you do that, you will have a real help in your own writing—a blueprint to publishable articles.

Magic Formula Plan

An especially popular method of organizing an article is sometimes called the Magic Formula plan. It has four distinct parts, i.e.: Lead, Slant, Body, and End.

As in any article, the purpose of the *Lead*—the first paragraph should be enough—is to lure the reader on. It is a device designed to cry out to the reader, "Here, friend, is something you can't afford to miss!" And the more quickly and forcefully your lead does this, other elements being equal, the better.

I have called the second part of a Magic Formula article *Slant*. This—the second paragraph—is a portion of the article which does not come from any book you read, any article you peruse, any interview you conduct. Instead, this is what *you* want to say about the subject you have introduced in your lead.

Suppose your subject is health. You know this subject is ancient. Therefore, if you are to sell your article, you must say something new about health.

So you sit down to plan paragraph two of the article. In it you are going to say something to attract the editor's attention. What can it be? This, indeed, is the vital question. This is the point at which you prove conclusively that you are—or are not—a writer. What can you do about this extremely important short paragraph?

Suppose you write: *We must protect our health.* You may elaborate on that theme in fifty or so well chosen words. Your English is perfect. There is impact to your finished prose. Yet you have flunked flatter than a flounder!

Why? Even morons know we must protect our health, and you have offered the reader nothing more than just that.

Try again. This time you write: *We're hearing too much about protection. One would think that we are a nation of invalids.*

Now this, at least, is something new. It has not been said a million times. It is not "old hat." It is bound to bring a reaction of a positive sort. This, then, is a possibility for an article. If you can build a sound argument to prove this point, if you can give the reader something that will actually help him, you are well on your way toward writing a Magic Formula article that will sell.

So, in your slant in the Magic Formula article you tell the reader what you propose to give him in the article. You give the direction to the article. You foreshadow some of the delights which he may find in the article—something he hasn't heard a thousand times before. This is promising reading. It will interest the editor first, then perhaps a million readers.

Do writers actually do this? They do. For instance, in a recently published article, the slant paragraph tells of an architect who designs homes to express the owners' personalities. In still another slant paragraph, the author gently scorns the idea of parents' insisting that their children take plenty of physical exercise. This is all but unimaginable. Yet the article sold to one of the better small magazines.

Neither of these slants, you will observe, is world-shaking but each one of them is original to a considerable degree. This, then, is a significant lesson for you. Refuse to write the trite. Give your articles an original slant. This can mean sales and sales and sales for you.

This brings us to the major portion of the article—the *Body*. In a Magic Formula planned article, the body is made up of two ingredients: (1). Facts, observations, and incidents; and (2). Interpretive sentences which emphasize the slant of your article. For example:

I have a friend whose grandmother will have no part or parcel of crowded stores during the Christmas shopping season. Instead, she keeps a list of the people she wishes to remember and distributes her presents throughout the year. A much-wanted chair for sun-bathing arrived in June with a card saying, "Merry Christmas from Grandmother." My friend declares that these unscheduled gifts are always a particularly delightful surprise.

I am not suggesting that everyone should send Christmas gifts in June. The point I would like to make is that an occasional detour from the well-marked highway of the ordinary to the byroad of individuality can be a healthy release from routine.

The italicized lines are the interpretive portion of the foregoing idea. This is the particular feature of the Magic Formula plan. In building the body of the Magic Formula article, you arrange the various items in order of ascending interest just as in the straight chronological method. Then, as frequently as you can within reason, you insert an interpretive sentence which will tend to emphasize your slant.

Too, if you wish to tantalize your readers, you may introduce an incident—or incidents—which tends to disprove your slant. The purpose of this is to inject the element of suspense into the article, to give to the fact piece some of the appeal of fiction. When you do this, you will —by the interpretive sentence at the end of the incident —show conclusively that the anecdote failed utterly to disprove your thesis.

And so to the final portion of the article—the *End.* This often becomes a short summary, or a roundup of what you have said. It should, however, contain one significant new fact. And it must end with impact—something that will leave the reader satisfied.

This is an especially effective method of article organization as you will note from the following example:

BUILD A NEW MENTAL IMAGE OF YOURSELF *

By William W. West

Recently, I visited a friend whose king-sized French poodle jumped on me, pawed me, and tried to curl up on my lap, although he hung over a yard at each end.

My friend shook his head. "Poor Voltaire. He still thinks of himself as a puppy."

Voltaire's inability to see himself as others see him is not a failing confined to the canine world. Many people have only a sketchy conception of themselves.

At a recent amateur theater guild audition, I watched a middle-aged, heavy-set woman try out for the part of a young, beautiful heroine. In counseling teen-agers, I've encountered many powerhouses chained by false images of themselves. At one time, I thought half the movies from Hollywood concerned the Mr. Meek who suddenly throws off his mental image, turns on the bandits, becomes a football hero, or swears at his mother-in-law.

Your mental image of yourself is the result of years of subtle conditioning through personal, family, and social experiences. Your actions and reactions build a mosaic that is *you*. This *mental image* is a little more difficult to alter than the movies would indicate—but it can be done.

A psychologist recently recognized the conditioning process when he refused an invitation to enter his exceptional four-year-old son in kindergarten. "Enroll Scott in kindergarten a year early? Absolutely not! He might be ahead of the other children intellectually—but his lack of coordination and his smaller size would make him dependent on the other children. If anything, I'll keep him out of school a year longer so that his first impression of himself in school will be that *he* is the leader!"

* Reprinted by permission of *Your Life.*

The psychologist's son, if he had started school a year younger than his classmates, might have developed a life-pattern of dependence. Similarily false mental images may sometimes induce frustration, repression, and apathy. Some socially unacceptable sexual behavior may be partially attributed to false mental images.

Although childhood conditioning has fashioned the picture each of us has of himself, there are some positive steps we can take to improve the mental images. These steps will help you.

1. Examine your mental image of yourself. Perhaps you don't know now what you think of yourself! Eastern philosophers spend years in self-examination. Psychiatrists begin psychoanalysis by fitting together the intricate fragments which reveal the subject's interpretation of himself. This first step is not an easy one—but look as dispassionately as possible at your personality, your character, your physical appearance, and your effectiveness as a parent, worker, lover, and friend. Insofar as you can determine, is your image in each case satisfactory? What does it lack?

2. Watch for the picture others seem to have of you. Remember that no one except *you* can know *you;* no one else can get inside your skin and determine what *you are.* And since you can't ever know exactly what others are thinking, don't worry too much about what you find. You can, however, detect some indication of others' thoughts by analyzing their conversation, attitudes, and relationships. It is important to try to get this picture, because the images others have of you sometimes influence your own mental outlook.

3. Choose the mental image of yourself which you feel would be effective in your life and identify yourself with it. This step is not easy. It involves examining realistically your abilities and limitations. But it can be done effectively. A former student recently told me, "I was always worried about money, so my mental image of myself included a picture of a cring-

ing little man with empty pockets. As I displaced this image, I felt almost a compulsion to get rid of the expenditures that were inducing the picture!"

4. Think positively about yourself. Say to yourself, "This is my old mental image of myself; this is my new one. This is what I must do." Replace an undesirable picture with a stimulating one; never leave a vacuum. Wishful thinking or envy soon fill a vacuum with bitterness. Feel confident that *you can do something* to improve.

Attempting to change one's mental image of oneself goes back to the thought of two philosophers: Socrates said, "Know thyself." Emerson said, "Trust thyself." Pragmatists tell us that truth is to be tested by the consequences of the belief. If you believe in a new *you,* and the belief results in desirable changes, who can say your belief is not true?

On these bases, knowing and trusting yourself, you can build a new mental image of yourself; a mental image that results in a better *you.*

Magic Formula Analysis

Let us look at this article in outline form as a means of learning to construct others according to the Magic Formula plan.

    I. Lead
       A. Dog incident
   II. Slant
       A. We see ourselves hazily
  III. Body
       A. Would-be actress
          1. Interpretive sentence
       B. Psychologist's son
          1. Interpretive sentence

    C. How we may improve
       1. Study ourselves
       2. Study what others think of us
       3. Select mental image for ourselves
       4. Think positively
IV. End
    A. Believe in a new you
       1. Interpretive sentence
    B. New fact
       1. This can result in a new you

This method of organizing an article is entirely sound. Every month thousands of articles planned in this manner appear in print. Yours may be among them if you learn this method well and practice it.

TRAIN-OF-THOUGHT METHOD

A third way to organize an article—the Train-of-Thought method—is best of all. You as a serious writer cannot afford to ignore this potent manner of assembling the various parts of an article. Thousands of writers utilize this plan almost exclusively.

Moreover, it will work well for anecdotes, book chapters, and even for books. With a full knowledge of this bit of writing technique, you can make your work truly forceful.

The Train-of-Thought method has four parts, i.e.: The Snowplow, Locomotive, Train of Cars, and Caboose. These occur in the order named. Let us examine these sections of the article one by one.

Snowplow—the initial paragraph of an article. Its function is to strike the reader with impact that will make him read on. This portion of the article, therefore, must be intriguing.

Locomotive—the second paragraph of an article organized according to this plan. It establishes clearly what the article offers the reader. The Locomotive leaves the reader with the feeling that he simply must see what else the article has to offer, and, therefore, must be even more intriguing than the Snowplow.

Train of Cars—the major portion of the article. In this part of the piece there will be many anecdotes, facts, and observations, each of which is a "car" in the Train of Cars.

In arranging the order of the "cars" in the Train of Cars, you will begin with the least interesting item you have to report. The next one will be more intriguing, and the next one even more so. This will continue until you reach the most dramatic incident of the entire article. This is the climax.

Caboose—the end of the article. Here you will inject one pertinent new fact—something that will have a considerable impact upon the reader. And you will end the article with absolute finality, seeing that it rings true all the way through.

Here is an example of a Train-of-Thought article:

AN ISLAND FOR EVERY MAN *

By Omer Henry

It's safe to say that every man, at least once in his life, has been seized by an urge for seclusion, for nature, for the Call of the Wild. Every man, in his innermost recesses, has desired to get away, to find a place where he can think—or not think,

* Reprinted by permission of *The Kiwanis Magazine* (April, 1959).

as the case may be. To work with his hands; to find unas-
sailable privacy; to possess one plot of ground where he alone
is master. Perhaps it's true that, as John Donne insisted, "No
man is an island." But it is equally certain that at one time
or another every man wants to own one.

It may be, therefore, a source of pleasure for some people
to know that if they really want an island they can have it.
Within the coastal and interior waterways of North America
are more than a million islands—most of them totally un-
inhabited and yet habitable—for sale at prices as low as $10
an acre. But even at prices that are not rock bottom, to buy
and convert an island to comfortable living can cost no more
than to buy a 50 by 80 foot lot in a well populated resort area,
often less.

The first important consideration in island-buying is location. Some folks want their island to be as close to home as
possible; others will talk about "getting away" and mean it.
If you intend to use your island during the summer months
only, Michigan, Minnesota, Wisconsin, Maine, Canada, and
the Thousand Islands section of the St. Lawrence are likely
places to look. Likewise, the coast of the Carolinas, Florida,
Alabama, Mississippi, or Louisiana provide a climate for year-
round or winter living.

Exactly what is the process of locating an island for sale—
one you would want to buy? Morris Burrie, Canadian islander,
says: "Since the Ontario wilderness appealed to me, I wrote to
the Department of Travel and Publicity, Parliament Building,
Toronto, for information. By return mail I had a bundle of
literature and maps of available islands."

Burrie studied the maps, which show the world's greatest
concentration of islands. He wanted a small, undeveloped
tract in a particular locale.

"I found several islands," he says, "which appeared to be
possible choices. I marked them on the maps. Then I went
on location."

Going "on location" for Burrie meant hiring a small airplane and flying over the islands he had checked on the map. "I could tell from the air," he says, "that an island was too rocky, too barren, too swampy, too far from the mainland, or that it was smooth, high enough above the waterline so it would not be flooded. I marked off on my map those islands which did not seem suitable for my purpose."

His next step was to make a personal inspection of each island that appeared from the air to be something in which he might be interested. After a week or so of walking over the islands, comparing each one with the others, and learning first-hand the actual condition of each, he decided on a three-acre plot of ground with a protected bay, tiny sand beach, and heavy growth of fir and birch.

Burrie's island is in an area where there are hundreds of lakes and thousands of islands. Moose, deer, and bear abound. Fishing is excellent. "And," Burrie says with zest, "not only is this an ideal vacation spot, but I am king of my island!"

South of the Canadian border, island hunters face a different situation. Few islands there remain property of the United States government. "Those under federal ownership," says Dwight F. Reetie of the Bureau of Land Management, "are often masses of rock, inaccessible, unsurveyed, subject to recurrent flood, not classified for disposal, or otherwise unavailable to people seeking vacation or residential areas."

The basic supplier of islands in the United States and coastal waters is the real estate agent. Therefore you should contact a realtor located in the locale where you wish to buy. Chambers of Commerce may be helpful to you in supplying names and addresses of such real estate dealers.

You may want to try out island living before investing in an island. If so, you may do this in any one of several ways, e.g.:

Isle Royale, a national park in the northwestern corner of

Lake Superior, offers a standing invitation to island prospectors. Nothing on wheels is allowed there, but 80 miles of trails are marked for hiking, and inland lakes—because they are so seldom fished—are among the best fishing locations in the country. Isle Royale also abounds with, of all things, moose. In the winter of 1912 a small herd went over 14 miles of ice from Canada to Isle Royale and now the herd numbers 500 or more.

Or, if you want something more primitive, you might try "roughing it" on an island of your own selection. Charles Helin of Detroit did that. He took several hunting and fishing trips into the Canadian wilds before he selected an island, which he likes so well he will not even identify it. It is an ideal spot, he says, and he proposes to keep it just that.

The cost of islands varies as much as their terrain, but occasionally one gets an island for almost nothing. That happened to Art Holiday, boatbuilder in an Eastern state. Locating a small, unoccupied island in a river, Holiday concluded that it must belong to the state.

If, he reasoned, the island were public domain, he had as much right to it as anyone. So he took possession of it. And for some months he lived in a tent on the island. As no one seemed to notice the fact, he built a small cabin among the trees.

Now he began to look upon this island as his property. However, he had no deed for it. That worried him a bit so he appealed to the courts, and by "squatters' rights" gained legal possession of the island. The cost to him—aside from court fees, labor, and building materials—was his daring. Few island hunters are that lucky—or that persistent.

Yet, if you are at least eighteen years old, you may homestead an island almost that cheaply. In Canada the cost will probably be about fifty cents an acre. It will be necessary that you reside on such a claim at least six months for each of three consecutive years and erect a habitable dwelling on it.

If you want to buy a Canadian island containing less than ten acres, the price may be $50 an acre. You also may buy one or more acres of a larger island at the same rate. Canada is glad to sell islands to Americans, but if an American wishes to homestead in Canada, he must declare his intention of becoming a Canadian citizen.

In an effort to obtain specific prices for islands in the United States and coastal waters, I queried real estate agents. They reported islands for sale at prices from $10 an acre for small, undeveloped plots to $300,000 for a 2500 acre Rocky Mountain empire in the middle of Flathead Lake, Montana.

A Bureau of Land Management prospectus announcing a sale—which closed in March 1958—of perhaps a hundred Florida islands included the following:

Lot 2 in Dixie county contains 3.66 acres appraised at $915. Sandy, high, well-drained, pine-hardwood forest along bank of Suwanee River. No roads on island. Good location for cabin site.

Lot 10 in Monroe county contains 0.94 acres appraised at $750. An island in the chain of Key Islands, 21 miles east of Key West, one-half mile north of Highway No. 1. Island has rock formation, supporting growth of dwarf mangrove. Water and electricity available.

It is possible in many parts of the United States to purchase an undeveloped island consisting of from one to five acres for $100 to $400. If the island is developed, the price is higher. But even so, it often happens that one finds fabulous island bargains. For instance:

Recently, to settle an estate, an agent offered a three-acre tract in the Thousand Islands rising twenty feet above high water level and containing a thirteen-room residence, well-furnished and solidly built of native stone and shingles—a palatial estate that cost $150,000 to build—for only $24,000.

It is a safe generalization that, dollar for dollar, you can get more for your money in island property than in any other type of real estate.

If it's true that island buying gives you more for your money, it is also true that getting the money in the first place is less easy. Real estate agents admit that it is more difficult to get a loan on an island than on other real property, the demand for islands being relatively small. But loans are available.

As if by way of balancing the loan difficulty, island taxes are far lower than those on comparable bits of real estate elsewhere. An island estate consisting of 106 acres and valued at $125,000, located in a very desirable location in Lake Superior, has an annual tax of only $162.20.

A ten-acre Canadian island having a house, boathouse, and nicely landscaped lawn, despite its $24,000 value, has an annual tax of only $55.31. Taxes on undeveloped islands are even lower than those quoted.

Experts generally advise that one purchase a developed island because the cost of transporting building materials, digging a well, constructing a dwelling and boatlanding—an absolute necessity—is apt to be deceptively high.

Just how high would those costs be? That depends on how you do the job. John and Barbara Cloud did it for one sum, George C. Boldt for another.

Cloud, a commercial photographer from Boston, wanted to get away from the day-to-day grind, to find a place where he could forget his job, relax, and enjoy life. He discovered Inner Green, an eight-acre island some 25 miles from Portland, Maine, and bought it for $1500. On it he and his wife built a three-room cottage, guest house, boat landing, and garden at a total cost—aside from labor—of $5,000.

"It's not elaborate," John says of his Lake Sebago island home. "But we can sit on the doorstep and catch bass, trout, and salmon. There are pheasant and partridge on the island and deer on the mainland. Wild rice and coontail planted along the shore attract duck and geese in season."

Thus the Clouds turned an undeveloped island into what they call "Our Paradise" for $6500. Others have done the job even more cheaply.

At the opposite extreme stands the story of Heart Island, one of the show places in the Thousand Islands. Purchasing it in 1900, George C. Boldt, multimillionaire, set out to construct the finest summer home in the entire region.

When he commissioned the architectural firm of Hewitt, Stevens, and Paist of Philadelphia to do the work, he told them that expense was a minor consideration. He shipped ton after ton of sand up the river for mortar, barge after bargeload of granite, and the finest white marble from Italy.

Each bedroom was, in reality, an apartment equipped with an attractive tapestry, brick fireplace, and a private bath which, in those days, was quite unusual. The castle was large enough to accommodate a hundred guests and their servants.

But Boldt did not stop at this. He even had the shape of the island changed to resemble that of an enormous human heart. "It was to be more than a summer home," historians tell us. "It was to be the heart of the colony that Boldt intended to establish there."

Then, before the mansion was completed, tragedy struck. Mrs. Boldt died, leaving her husband heartbroken. And, as he had undertaken this project for her, this was the ruination of his dream. He never wanted to see the castle again. By telegram he stopped all work on it.

It was never finished and no one has ever lived in it. Birds and bats have taken up housekeeping in its dusty halls, spiders run their webs over the marble fireplaces, and boys toss stones through the costly plate glass windows. The cost? Something like $3,000,000!

Most islanders get more from their investment than did Mr. Boldt, however. "You don't realize," says Charley Hanes, St. Louis businessman, "what an island can mean until you've been on one for a time. Even then it's hard to explain."

His eyes suddenly take on a dreaminess. "There's a kind of peace and quiet, a feeling that all's well, which settles over me the minute I step on my island. My worries disappear like magic. I get into fishing togs, crush a shapeless hat on my head, pick up my rod and reel, and suddenly life is beautiful."

A Detroit assembly-line worker puts it like this: "You wouldn't believe the peaceful feeling my island gives me. On it I'm isolated from the world without building a fence or blocking a road. I get out my axe and chop firewood, I fish for food, and fix my own meals. It's worth a hundred vacations at a fancy resort."

Ed Messinger of the Thousand Islands says: "Here I find everything I want—tranquility and exciting country. The fishing is unexcelled. Smallmouth bass—the fightingest fish pound-for-pound in the world—is the target for thousands of sportsmen during the season."

As he talks, excitement plays on his face, in his eyes and voice. "Then," he adds, "we have the great northern pike; in late summer and fall the big ones, the giant muskellunge, tiger of the river. You must have patience and sturdy gear, but if your luck holds, it can pay off with 60 pounds of fighting monster. Man, that's living!"

At the opposite end of the country, Bert Beale is equally enthusiastic about Vaca, one of the Key islands. "Vaca," he says, "is a coral limestone inlet bathed by the clear tropic seas of the Atlantic and Gulf of Mexico.

"Among the fissured coral lurk giant crawfish, Florida lobster, crabs, shrimp, and hundreds of varieties of mollusks. Inhabiting the reefs are black porcupine sea urchins, sea fans, and plumes that wave graceful wands of tan and purple. In the rainbow-hued waters are more than 600 varieties of salt-water quarry."

It is small wonder that Beale gets poetic about the charms of Vaca island. "Out on the ocean flats," he declares, "are bonefish, an angler's greatest light-tackle game! In short, Vaca is the nearest thing to a South Seas atoll straddling a United States highway!"

And so it is with thousands of islanders—homesteaders to multimillionaires, retired men to harried executives, truck drivers to the Secretary of State. Far from being bored with the Old Rat Race, these men are really enjoying life. Their islands are material aids to that end.

And, finally, an island is not expendable. You may use it year after year, then sell it—probably for a price greater than the one you paid.

"Dollar for dollar," says islander Charles Handley, "it is doubtful if any other investment will add as much zest to your life as a private island."

A private island is a world apart, where making the top dollar becomes wholly unimportant and the sound of white-capped surf restlessly chafing the beach is as peaceful as the silence of the aromatic pines. And if you really want it, it's yours.

Train-of-Thought Article Analysis

Quite naturally it is more difficult to organize a long article than a short one. Therefore, I have used a full-length feature for this illustration. If you fully understand how it is fitted together, you should have little difficulty with your own.

The first step in organizing an article is to build its backbone. Here is the backbone of "For Every Man an Island":

I. Snowplow
   A. Do you want an island
II. Locomotive
   A. You may have a private island
III. Train of Cars
   A. How
      1. Location
      2. Selection
      3. Canadian islands
      4. United States islands
   B. Try out island living
      1. Isle Royale
      2. Charles Helin's method
   C. Cost of islands
      1. Art Holiday
      2. Homesteading in Canada
      3. Buying in Canada
      4. Realtors' report
      5. Bureau of Land Management's report
      6. Island bargains
      7. Taxes
      8. Inner Green
      9. Heart Island
   D. Rewards
      1. Charley Hanes
      2. Detroit islanders
      3. Ed Messinger
      4. Bert Beale
IV. Caboose
   A. For all types of men
   B. New fact
      1. Not expendable

    C. Matchless peace
       1. Yours if you want it

Such an outline not only gives order to your work but also tells you without fail where a particular bit of information fits best in the article. This enables you to save a tremendous amount of time and to present your story with real impact. In short, an outline can pay you really big cash dividends.

REWARDS OF PLANNING

Each of the foregoing articles is a compact, unified bit of writing, an effective presentation of pertinent material. And each one "comes off" in a thoroughly satisfactory manner.

There is no hocus-pocus, no inspiration, no mystery about organizing an article well. You simply give it appeal, direction, set forth the necessary evidence to establish your contention, keep the interest rising to a definite climax, and then close the article in a convincing and satisfying manner.

This is a mechanical process, a sort of building procedure. You assemble the various parts of the article in such a way as to give the greatest possible impact to what you want your article to say.

Thus, the proper organization of your article can simplify your writing, help convince an editor that you are a competent professional, and bring you more and bigger sales. What more could you ask?

Chapter VIII

PICTURES INCREASE PROFITS

YOUR BUSINESS as a writer is not only to sell each article you write but to sell it for the highest possible amount. Luckily, by giving a bit of thought to the matter, you can, with surprisingly little effort, vastly increase your writing income.

To do this you must realize that an editor pays you not on an hourly or weekly basis but by piece work. If you deliver to him an acceptable article, he pays you a given sum; but if, with the article, you also offer him suitable illustrations, he will buy them, too. The purchase price for the pictures is often as much, and sometimes even more, than the amount paid for the article itself. Therefore, you should give serious thought to the supplying of good photographs to illustrate your own articles. This is far easier to do than you may suspect. A great many writers sell photographs to illustrate their own articles. So can you.

There are two methods by which you may obtain photographs with which to illustrate your articles, i.e.: (1). Get them from others, or (2). Take them yourself.

It may surprise you to know that throughout the country there are millions of photographs from which you may choose illustrations for your articles. These pictures concern every subject under the sun. Some of them are black and white, others are in color, and all of them are of professional quality. Best of all, a majority of them are free!

Public relations departments of industrial concerns, governmental offices, press agents for celebrities, and even private individuals have fabulous picture libraries. Your problem is to learn these sources. A bit of elementary reasoning can help you. For instance: Suppose you were writing an article about sod houses which dotted the states of Kansas and Nebraska in the nineteenth century. How would you get suitable photographs with which to illustrate the article?

I felt that the historical societies of those states would be logical sources, and, therefore, I wrote to the Nebraska State Historical Society explaining my need. Almost by return mail I had a dozen or so glossy 8x10 photographs from which I could obtain not only usable but excellent illustrations for my article.

In addition the Photograph Librarian wrote to me: "We are enclosing also our Educational Leaflet No. 3. This gives some description of sod house building and other phases. For a more detailed discussion we might refer you to Everett Dick's *Sod House Frontier* which should be readily available . . . Also Cass G. Barns' *The Sod House.* . . ." I have often received additional information and suggestions of this type when I asked for photographs.

Writing of the contemporary scene, let us say you need photographs of aluminum fabrication. It well may be that the Kaiser Aluminum and Chemical Corporation, 1924 Broadway, Oakland, California, can supply precisely the photographs you want.

Should it be fishing and wildlife photographs you need, write to the U.S. Fish and Wildlife Service, P.O. Box 128,

College Park, Maryland. Mr. Rex Gary Schmidt, Chief, in charge of the visual information section, has an extensive picture file on this subject. Almost all of the departments of the U.S. government maintain extensive photographic files. In some instances you may obtain prints free from these sources. Other agencies make a nominal charge— from 50 cents to a dollar—for an 8x10 glossy of professional quality. The Library of Congress and National Archives are especially useful in supplying photographs of famous individuals and historical events.

No matter what your subject, in the United States or abroad you can very likely obtain free photographs suitable for use in illustrating your article. Learn these sources. Build a photograph source index of your own. It can mean many an added dollar in your bank account.

Shooting Your Own Photographs

However valuable you may find "cold storage" photographs, they can only supplement—never replace—those made to illustrate a particular article. Therefore, if you are a businesslike writer, you will want to learn to shoot photographs with which to illustrate your articles. Before you can consistently sell your photographs to magazines, you must become a reasonably competent photographer. This, contrary to the general impression, is not difficult. The initial step is to gain at least a rudimentary understanding of photographic equipment—cameras in particular. If you understand the limitations of your camera and have perfect conditions under which to work, you can make publishable pictures with the cheapest camera. However, you almost never have perfect working conditions. Therefore, you will be wise to buy a camera which will compensate, to a degree, for the lack of ideal shooting conditions.

This calls for a consideration of cameras, three types in particular:

1. Press camera

By "press camera" I refer to such cameras as Speed Graphic 4x5, Crown Graphic 4x5, Busch Pressman 4x5, etc. These have f/4.7—or faster—lens and shutter speeds up to 1/1000 of a second. The cost of such a camera may be between $150 and $500, but it will last a lifetime. In my opinion this is the best possible camera for you. With it you can photograph just about anything at any time, and that, to you as a writer, is worth much.

2. Reflex camera

Your second best choice of camera is the reflex—such as the Rolleicord or Rolleiflex. These use roll film—120 or 620 in general—and give a $2\frac{1}{4}$x$2\frac{1}{4}$ negative. The lenses are f/3.5 or faster, and the shutter speeds are up to 1/400 of a second.

Light in weight, these cameras are easily handled and convenient to carry. Also, they have a ground glass finder in which you can see the image which will be reflected on your film. This enables you to make certain that your picture is in focus before you snap the shutter. Such a camera may cost from $25 to $400 or more. It is an excellent camera for the beginning writer to use.

3. Candid camera

Although the candid camera—the 35mm type—uses small film, it is not a toy. Well constructed, entirely professional in quality, with proper care it will last a lifetime, and expert photographers obtain excellent results with it. Because of its size, the 35mm camera is the most convenient of all cameras to carry. It is light in weight, and a single spool of film will contain from 20 to 36 exposures. This makes it by far the least expensive of all cameras suitable for writers.

Often the 35mm camera lens is faster than that of the press or reflex camera, and the shutter speed may range up to 1/2000 of a second! Its prime fault is that the film is so small. If you wish to make an 8x10 enlargement from 35mm film, the magnification is so great that the print will be fuzzy unless the camera was in exact focus when the shutter was snapped. You can't, of course, sell an out-of-focus picture and you are likely, therefore, to find the candid camera the least desirable of the three types of cameras discussed here.

You may use either black and white or color film in any of these cameras. In buying a camera, you should consider carefully the fact that almost no editor will object to color shots being $2\frac{1}{4}$x$2\frac{1}{4}$ or larger, but a majority of magazines —as of this writing—will not buy 35mm transparencies.

As there are fewer markets for color than black and white pictures, the latter are consequently far easier to sell. It all adds up to this: Your chances with black and white pictures, other elements being equal, are better than with color shots.

PHOTOGRAPHER'S GROUND RULES

You must, of course, learn to recognize a publishable picture. This involves, principally, two considerations or ground rules for publishable photographs:

1. See that your picture actually illustrates your article.

To understand the meaning of this rule, you need only pick up any magazine which is illustrated by photographs.

For instance, here on my desk is the current issue of *Dodge News,* the travel magazine. The lead article is called "Family Shellfishing Is Fun!"

What are the pictures? One shows two children age 10 or so standing by a crab trap with water in the background. Each child is holding a crab. And the caption reads: "Look at those succulent beauties! These youngsters got great results with their crab trap in State of Washington waters."

Other pictures are as pertinent to the article. Each of these has a definite bearing on the subject under discussion. And each picture tends to make the sport of shellfishing more alluring.

2. Offer editors action photographs.

This means that you will photograph something happening which is pertinent to the article. There are exceptions to this rule, but basically it is a sound guiding principle.

3. Get your camera as close as possible to the subject.

Editors like plenty of detail in the pictures. Recently an editor, in telling me the kind of a picture he wanted for a particular article, said, "Fill up the frame with the people. Show their faces, their hands, what they are doing. Give me the details in this picture." This is a sound rule to follow.

4. Try to get as much contrast as possible in your pictures.

You will do this by including objects which will show up as black or white in a black and white photograph. If you are working with color, get into the picture a strong primary color—red, yellow, blue. These help to make the picture striking.

5. Photograph only those things which you want to show

in the picture. That is, keep the photograph uncluttered and simple. Keep out of it things which do not pertain to the article.

6. Try to find an unusual angle to shoot the ordinary picture. This may give it a certain freshness.

7. Begin at the beginning of the activity you are illustrating and take several shots of each step in sequence. If it is not an activity you are photographing, then make several exposures of each unusual facet of the subject, whatever it may be. This procedure will enable you to make a good selection for your editor when submitting the pictures with your article.

8. Make sure that your camera's eye—the lens—is really clean before you shoot a picture.

9. If your subject is a person, place him in the shade with his back to the sun. A newspaper used as a reflector helps prevent the deep shadows which always show when you photograph someone in the strong sunlight.

10. Finally, always remember, a pretty girl in a picture is probably responsible for more sales than any other single element.

SELLING ILLUSTRATED ARTICLES

How do you begin? A splendid way to begin is to take a vacation—with plenty of film. It really doesn't matter where, as long as you are alert to what is around you. You must *see* the things around you and record them on film. A compelling set of facts can sell more pictures than the best photography, but if you are really professional, you will produce a fascinating story and a good set of photographs. That unbeatable combination is well within the range of your abilities.

I think that the picture taking is far simpler than the article writing. If you are in doubt, here is an example from my current files:

Last fall while on vacation, I spent a night at Colby, Kansas. Upon emerging from my motel the next morning, I discovered the morning newspaper stuffed into the handle of my car door. Attached to this newspaper by a small rubber band was a 3x5 card advertising the Pyramid Restaurant.

This seemed to me a good means of attracting customers, one which other restaurants might profitably use. So I photographed it, went to the Pyramid for a good breakfast, and obtained a bit of information about the place.

Back home again, I processed the film, sent an 8x10 glossy print with a caption to *Food Service* magazine. Shortly thereafter I had this letter from the editor:

Dear Mr. Henry:

The photograph and item you sent us on the Pyramid Restaurant in Colby, Kansas are interesting tidbits. For this we are willing to send you a large check of $5. Then we will have the problem of wondering what to do with our purchase.

We would rather keep this little thing on file hoping you would send us 8 or 10 more tidbits of a similar nature for which we would be more than pleased to send you a somewhat larger check in the amount of $100.

It seems to us that a group of ideas like this—half of which would be illustrated with a photograph while maybe half would not need illustration—could make an interesting feature. All of the ideas should be aimed at food service merchandising and should be practical, simple, and inexpensive as this Pyramid Restaurant idea certainly is. What is your choice—a check for $5 or one for $100?

Enclosed are several copies of *Food Service* magazine to give you some idea regarding our style.

Cordially,

In reply, I told the editor I would send him an article, which I did, with pictures.

A few days after I sent this article to editor Myers, I had this reply:

Dear Mr. Henry:

We like your "Roadside Goldmine" [my title] story and are happy to accept it for *Food Service* magazine.

Enclosed is our check for $100.

Cordially,

Was it superb photographs that sold this story? Indeed it was not. These pictures were far from spectacular. But they were good, clear shots which illustrated well the point the article made. Yet, anyone with a fair knowledge of photography could have taken them.

Conclusion: You need not be an expert photographer to sell photographs to magazines. You must, however, produce pictures which forcefully illustrate your article. When you do that, your pictures will sell.

WHO BUYS WHAT?

There are many ways to find the answer: The writers' magazines carry lists of market tips, but for information on picture markets, any writer needs another publication— *Gebbie Press House Magazine Directory*. In this publication you will find listed the picture requirements of more than 3,000 house organs. Here is a terrific market for pictures which you may take any day in any part of the country. Suppose you let Con Gebbie, who knows more about this business than any other man alive, describe this market and give you some tips on how to make real money with your camera.

THERE'S GOLD IN HOUSE ORGANS *

By Con Gebbie

If I were a free-lancer, instead of a publisher, I would do nothing but shoot pictures for house organs. I would make between $5,000 and $15,000 a year, depending upon the amount of time I spent at it. And I am just a fair photographer.

Five or $15,000 a year shooting for house organs alone—impossible? Not at all. I know, because I was a free-lancer who actually did it—and now I'm one of the hundreds of house organ publishers who buy pictures. But I'll point out one thing right off: You must be more than a photographer to get any place in this huge field. (3,000 major house organs, over 100,000,000 circulation!)

You have to be a businessman first, a researcher second, a writer third, and somewhere down the line, a photographer. You have to be able to produce clean negatives and sharp prints, true—but this market doesn't buy photography simply because it is good photography. The market has a single track mind—it buys product-application photos by the thousands and, with rare exceptions, turns down everything else.

A product-application photo, simply stated, is a shot that shows either the product or the service provided by the company whose house organ will use it. That's a simple definition,

* Reprinted with permission of Con Gebbie, author, and *U.S. Camera*.

but if you lose sight of it, you'll fall flat on your face in this market.

Free-lancers who make good money in the house organ field know five basic, sound rules:

1. Nearly every one of the 3,000-odd major house organs published in the U.S. will buy pictures—if the shots show their products or services in action.

2. A good product-application picture or photo story can be sold up to 15 or more different times.

3. House organs do not demand exclusive or "first rights" shots. (They have no competition from other publications, so they don't care if your shot has been published a hundred times elsewhere.)

4. General-interest photo stories have only the faintest hope of selling—and then only to a small group of general publications where competition is terrific.

5. Only the businessman-photographer who knows what to do with his shot after it is taken will make a go of it in this field, and he'll do handsomely.

The product-application photo demands a certain type of editorial thinking which, strangely enough, many highly experienced and successful photographers in other fields never seem to grasp.

For example: Two photographers recently covered the opening of a sewage disposal plant in New Jersey. Both took the standard over-all shot. One photographer sold it to the local newspaper and then ran out of ideas. The second photographer has already sold it *seven times,* and is just beginning to scratch the surface.

Both men took the same product-application shot. The first man thought like the average photographer and made one sale. The second man took his shot, *forgot photography*—and became a businessman.

Where do you find product-application photos? They are

right in front of your camera lens all the time, no matter where you are. If you live on a farm, and if you have imagination, you can make a neat amount just photographing farm machinery and equipment at work—in fields, in the dairy barn, in . . . well, you name it.

If you live in a small town, you are lucky because you have literally hundreds of product-application stories right at hand —and practically no competition. Walk down Main Street this afternoon with product-application eyes.

Whose gasoline station is on the corner? A possible sale to the big oil company back east. Show the local owner doing some company-approved method of service. (Not that the editor back east doesn't already have hundreds of servicing shots—he does. But he doesn't have one from your town, and the new locale and new face will give him a fresh reason for re-emphasizing a point the company insists he run often.)

Whose drug store is a few doors down the street? If it's a chain store—another likely sale. And inside, whose products are being sold? (The number of different companies with house organs supplying that one store would astound you!) Arrange with the proprietor to show him making a sale of a product to a customer—a product whose company has a house organ. Again, imagine the staggering number of possible product-application shots you can take in this one spot alone!

The proprietor, the customer, the display—but a different product each time. Two hours of shooting should keep you busy for a week just merchandising those prints off to market.

If you live in a medium-size city, you have all these possibilities and many more because the chances are good that at this very moment, some kind of construction is going on. Have you ever considered how many different products and services go into the construction of even a small building?

Ground is being broken for the foundation. Whose earth-moving equipment is on the job? A likely sale to the company that built that equipment. (Let me again point out that the company's editor already has hundreds of on-the-job photos in his files—but he does not have one of his equipment *on this job*. That's the important thing because that editor must rack his brain each month for new and different ways to show his product in action.)

A talk with the general contractor or purchasing agent in charge will turn up a whole series of possible picture-and-caption shots. Let's name just a few:

Whose concrete is being poured? How many firms are involved in the wiring? What kind of equipment? Who supplies the steel framework? The roofing material? The paint inside and out?

What special construction material is being used . . . glass blocks . . . decorative brick . . . insulation material . . . special paneling . . . window frames . . . etc.

Are floors covered with linoleum . . . or what? Who supplies the communications equipment . . . who installs it? The mirrors in the wash rooms . . . the plumbing . . . the antiseptic and cleaning material . . . the lighting fixtures?

Whose office equipment will be used? . . . typewriters, office desks, filing cabinets, tabulating machines, check writers, postage machines . . . whose business forms and bookkeeping systems?

What delivery trucks are used . . . who has the fuel contract . . . what kind of heating equipment is being installed . . . refrigeration and air conditioning . . . fire prevention equipment?

Raw materials come into the factory . . . how many different kinds, and how many suppliers? The finished product is shipped in some firm's boxes and cartons. Whose?

The possibilities of such stories are limited only by the free-lancer's imagination—and industry.

And it is at this point that the average free-lancer trained in other fields fails so badly. He simply cannot visualize all the products and services which go into even the simplest of ventures—and he doesn't realize that somewhere, someplace, a house organ editor would welcome fresh picture-and-caption material of his products in use.

Now that you can see the immense possibilities of product-application photos, let's consider a few mechanical details.

When you cover a store opening, visit the bank (think of all the different business machines there!), cover a new building, go to a farm, or shoot the construction of a new road, plan your shooting so that you can get at least a dozen or more different product-application pictures in one session. (You'll never make any money shooting just one or two shots for one or two magazines—then calling it a day. It's hard work if you want to make hard cash!)

A good basic rule is to take one over-all shot, then move in to get the product in action. In most cases, it is best to submit at least two shots and two captions. The over-all caption explains the locale, names, addresses, general description. The second caption gives details about the product's *reason for being in the picture*. The reason might be: A novel display, a new and different use (consider the number of different uses for a Dixie cup!), a strange location, a different application, newly introduced, or—more likely—another instance of how widely the product is used.

Do not waste time writing a detailed story. Give the facts simply and cleanly in about 50 words. The house organ editor knows his product much better than you do and he'll do the writing if you'll give him the basic facts.

Your prints should be 8x10 on glossy paper, dried either glossy or on a blotter. Attach the caption to the center of the back of the print with rubber cement. Include your name, address, and the words, *"For publication at your usual rates."*

There is no general rule for payment in the house organ

field. Some magazines pay as little as $3.50 a picture-and-caption; the majority pay between $15 and $30, and a few pay from $75 to $100. But even the minimum is quite good—if you sell it over and over again.

There is no cut-and-dried formula for finding the best magazines to shoot for. Generally speaking, the products shown in your pictures will dictate your markets. After several months experimentation, you'll find a certain number of publications which like your work and which can be depended upon for checks on a fairly regular basis—if you keep shooting.

Consider these your rent-and-overhead payers, and go to work merchandising the hundreds of other magazines. Some will buy only once a year, perhaps—but in sum total these sales should amount in quantity to several times your so-called rent-payer sales. These magazines will give you your real profit, and your profit will depend entirely upon what kind of businessman you are, how much ingenuity you have, and how well you have trained yourself in the product-application photo field.

Comment

The foregoing are but a few of the facts on this subject. In addition, there is the exclusive photograph which you can occasionally make. There is the cover photograph, the picture story, and the re-sale of your pictures over and over again. As years go by, this can add up to a rather sizable amount.

Yes, if you are really a business-minded writer, learn to use a camera. With it you can easily double your writing income. More, you can have fun doing so. Having fun making money is a hard-to-beat combination.

Chapter IX

THAT EXTRA FIVE PERCENT

••

THERE are five steps which will help you make your article manuscript "professional" and put it into the salable category. These are suggestions which you can and should follow with every article you write.

CHOOSING A TITLE

First, you should give most careful attention to the title of your article. This is the first thing the editor is going to read when your manuscript reaches his desk, and if your title fails to interest him, you are off to a bad start. But if you give him a title which whets his interest, you've won round one in the battle for an editorial check.

What is a good title?

We may define it as a short phrase—perhaps even a word —which immediately sets up in the reader's mind a desire to learn more about the subject. It must appeal to his imagination. It must offer him something of real interest, and it should epitomize the theme of the article.

How does one go about writing such a title?

Look at the titles in the magazine to which you hope to sell your article. See how intriguing they are. Read the articles and understand how apt these titles are. Do they do something to your imagination, or are they flat, dull, uninspiring?

Perhaps an example would be helpful. Let us suppose that you have written a travel article about the White House. You could choose as your title "The White House." That certainly identifies your subject matter. But is it inviting? Would you read an article carrying that prosaic title? I doubt it. You know about the White House. You have read articles or books on this subject and perhaps you have even seen it, walked through it. This title is dull and holds no lure whatsoever for the reader:

You are looking for something that will offer the reader a reward for reading your article. As he reads the article, he notes that you have pointed out that the White House is far more than the home of our Presidents. The White House is the center of the really great actions of our country over the years. It is, indeed, the very *heart* of the nation.

That phrase, you think, may be the right title for your article—"Heart of the Nation." Let us examine it. What, the reader would wonder, is the heart of the nation? We know that it fits the article, that it would arouse the curiosity of the reader. That is what a title should do, and we, therefore, decide to use it.

The Lead

From the title, the editor's eyes go in a flash to the lead of your article. This is your showcase. It is your job to put into that showcase items which will attract the editor. You are going to do this by offering the editor in an effective style something which he will believe is going to be of real interest to his readers.

Suppose you have written an article about the California

boys who put together a contraption which became the
basis for the sport known as karting. You write as your
lead:

A few years ago a couple of California boys built a miniature
automobile. It had four small wheels, a steel pipe frame, a
sheet metal body of sorts, a small gasoline motor, and a few
other odds and ends.

Now that tells the facts—facts which could be intriguing. But does that paragraph make you care about
what these boys did? Does it even make you wonder about
them?

Not very likely. This dull recital of a few flat facts carries no apparent significance. This paragraph fails to stir
your imagination, so you toss the magazine aside. The
trouble is the showcase lacks sparkle, allure.

So let's see if we can write a paragraph on this subject,
a paragraph which would cause you to read on. We might
tackle it in this way:

Three short years ago a couple of ingenious boys in southern
California performed a near miracle.

This lead about a "near miracle" means that the author
has something very rare to report. Precisely what, we wonder, did these ingenious boys do?

This lead, then, is a showcase which attracts attention.
It invites further reading. It is something that draws the
reader on, and it is a satisfactory lead for such an article.

How can you learn to write such leads?

You do it by considering the intriguing elements in your

article and deliberately offering to the reader enough in paragraph one to lure him on.

When you do this, your editor is going to say, "Here is a writer who can at least write an interesting lead. Let's see if he can keep it up." And this means that you have won round two in your battle for that editorial check.

The Anecdote

Your third check point is far more important than either the title or the lead. In fact, it is hardly an exaggeration to say that your article will stand or fall depending upon your handling of the anecdote.

Modern articles are often a series of anecdotes tied together with proper connectives and bits of interpretative writing. Here are a few suggestions designed to help you give your anecdotes the professional touch. Before you can use an anecdote in an article, you must find it, and that can be most difficult.

Some time ago I was gathering material for an article concerning a taxi company in Washington, D.C. The subject was dull. Every driver I interviewed had the same story: He went to work early each morning, drove carefully all day, seldom had an accident, and went home when the day was done.

This, I realized, would never sell my article. I must inject into it something far more intriguing than run-of-the-mine stuff before an editor was going to reach for his checkbook, which was my objective.

I kept on searching for the story which would lift my article into the realm of salable material. Finally, after listening to another routine story from Bill, a driver, I said:

"Bill, you've been a cab driver here for years. Surely you've had some exciting experiences while on the job."

He only shook his head. "None I can recall."

It was not, I felt, that he was uncooperative. He simply did not remember any incidents that would help to enliven my article. What he needed, I told myself, was a small charge of TNT in his brain. I tried to supply that element with these words:

"Bill, this is Washington, D.C., the capital of the United States, the greatest country on earth. Here we have Senators, Ambassadors, movie actors and actresses now and then, and even Kings and Queens on occasion. Here we have the President himself. It would seem to me that a man driving a cab as long as you have been would have had some experience with at least one of these famous people."

Bill smiled. "Well," he admitted, "I did have an experience with one of them." The smile broadened. "What an experience!"

"Good!" I exclaimed with pleasure. The TNT was beginning to work. "Tell me about it." And he told me a truly remarkable story. In my article* it appears in these words:

A Washington taxi driver named Bill Pinkney got the thrill of his lifetime one evening just because he conscientiously observes the safety rules of his employer, the Lincoln Cab Association.

Cruising in a brand-new Mercury along Connecticut Avenue shortly after the 1952 national election, with his wife, Mamie, in the front seat, Bill cluck-clucked in horror when another

* Reprinted by permission from *Fine Cars*, June, 1958.

driver executed a screaming U-turn just in front of him in the middle of the block.

Its purpose was to pick up two distinguished-looking men who were standing on the curb. But they deliberately ignored the taxicab cowboy. Instead, they signaled Bill to come around and pick them up.

"Oh!" gasped Mamie under her breath as they got into the cab.

"Tilden Street," said one of the men. "4801."

Pinkney eased his car into the traffic and kept his eyes straight ahead. That address was one of the best known in the nation's capital.

Presently one of the men spoke. "I guess we should tell these people who we are."

"We know one of you," said Mamie.

The man laughed. "Which one?"

Mamie turned to the dark-haired youngish man who had given Bill his address. "You," she said, "are our new Vice President."

Mr. Nixon and his companion, the New York newspaperman named Bert Andrews, seemed to relax as Pinkney drove on his careful way, chatting about the new Mercury, its smoothness, and how they detested wild-man cab drivers.

"When I stopped," Bill Pinkney relates, "the Vice President invited my wife and me to see his house. It was beautiful with elegant furniture and big mirrors, as clean and sparkling as my new car. Almost anything can happen in Washington, but I don't think we'd have had that thrill but for the training that made me a careful driver."

Careful driving—safety—was the theme of my article. And this anecdote fit it perfectly. This one incident, I feel, cinched the sale of this article.

You must do the same in your articles. Keep looking for the right anecdote to meet the requirements of your article; it can help you tremendously toward a sale.

An Almost-Good-Enough Anecdote

If you have an anecdote that is almost good enough, but does not quite please you, improve it. Often that is merely a matter of presentation. Let us use an actual example:

My husband, a famous scientist, frequently takes me to social functions attended by celebrities. On many occasions I have to grope for an adequate reply to someone's well-meant question, "And what do you do?" It seems that, because I am present with such a group of big-wigs, they assume I must be a person of considerable importance.

Then, for me to admit that I am only a housewife—which is true—is a distinct anticlimax. But, because I am unwilling to prevaricate, I have found myself in many an embarrassing situation.

A few days ago I attended such a luncheon. Dozens of important people were there and, as usual, a well-meaning gentleman asked me the inevitable question, "And what do you do?"

"Me?" I replied. Then inspiration came. "Oh, I raise boys."

Diagnosis

That is not a bad anecdote. It is logical, understandable, and fairly well presented. It even has a rather good final line. But it doesn't quite "come off."

What can we do to improve it?

First, we must decide precisely what is wrong with it as it stands. In my opinion it

1. Is verbose.

2. Can have more suspense.
3. Can be made far more vivid.
4. Can be made much more satisfying.

Cure

Get to the point of the anecdote more quickly than in the above draft. To do that you must do a bit of analyzing. Here are the facts with which we propose to deal:

An ordinary housewife is embarrassed at being asked by celebrities what she does. She hates to admit the truth —that she is just an ordinary housewife. Yet she is too honest to prevaricate.

Now, let us put those facts into a single, short sentence:

I have long looked for an answer to the question, "What do you do?" more adequate than, "I'm just a housewife."

This presents the situation with reasonable conciseness. I think we can improve it, though, as it does not give all the facts we want it to contain. So we try again:

As the wife of a noted scientist, I often meet top celebrities. When they ask me, as they frequently do, "What do you do?" I am reluctant to admit that I am just an ordinary housewife.

This is clear and it gives the situation—an understandable, convincing one—but it is too long; it contains a number of excessive words and ideas. Let's try again, this time cutting it to the very bone.

I have long looked for an answer to the question, "What do you do?" more adequate than, "I'm just an ordinary housewife."

This is concise. It is direct and interesting. Yet, it does not quite please me. For the moment, however, we shall accept it.

And since we found that cutting improved the beginning of this anecdote, let's try it as we progress. Our yardstick shall be: Is this word, this idea really necessary? If it isn't, we'll discard it.

One day I was surrounded at luncheon by illustrious people doing all sorts of marvelous things when one of these men—a Broadway producer—popped the annoying question.

Half of our verbiage has fallen away, and the incident moves with direction, interest, and we find ourselves racing on to see what happens next.

We try for more of the same. We write:

Suddenly I had an inspiration. "I raise boys," I answered.

Again this method of writing shows up in a favorable light. We conclude that there really is merit in conciseness.

But this is not enough. We must keep this going—going ahead to a satisfying end. And there must never be a lull in interest. So we bring in a brief, understandable line of dialogue.

"Really?" he asked. "Do you manage an orphanage?"

This is a logical guess in view of what the woman has said. But if we leave the story there, it is "cold potatoes." It is also "cold potatoes" if we permit the woman to say that she runs an orphanage.

Too, the answer must be honest, short, and apt. It

must fit what has gone before, and, if possible, it should have a touch of wit.

That is a difficult assignment. But we are writers, and we must face tough problems if we are to produce forceful prose. So we consider what we have written, see how we can improve it. Then, suddenly, we get a tremendous inspiration. We write:

I have long looked for an answer to the question, "What do you do?" more adequate than, "I'm just a housewife."

One day I was surrounded at luncheon by illustrious people doing marvelous things, when one of the men—a Broadway producer—asked the above question. I had an inspiration. "I raise boys," I answered authoritatively.

"Really?" he asked. "Do you manage an orphanage?"

"Oh, no," I replied blithely. "I'm in business for myself." *

Comment

This is what Milly H. Beatie did with this situation. As a result, she sold the anecdote to *The Reader's Digest's* "Life in These United States" for $100.

This shows rather clearly what you must do with a bit of writing that is almost good enough for publication. Diagnose the ailments and treat them one by one. Always deal with small units individually—never with the entire article. The results are likely to be truly spectacular.

When you have learned to write the anecdote well, you are within a stone's throw of writing the article well.

CLIMAX

Step number four on the check list is the one most often ignored, and yet it is so important that its omission can,

* Reprinted by permission of the author and *The Reader's Digest.*

and often does, prevent a sale. Conversely, it can, and quite frequently does, cinch a sale.

What is this element? Climax.

If you hope to sell your article, be sure it has a strong and—if possible—thrilling climax. This can be a most effective selling point. Precisely what is a climax? Why is it so important? How can you build a strong climax that will help you sell your article? A climax in non-fiction is comparable to climax in fiction. There the writer sets up a situation, brings a lovable proponent against a set of circumstances. Then the writer does something else that is tremendously important. *He involves the reader.* He does this by building the hero into such a person that the reader *wants* him to win.

Now the proponent meets all kinds of obstacles. These grow worse and worse as the story progresses. The hero is a courageous individual who battles for his objective, but unmistakably the odds are terribly against him. One turn after another puts the hero into a more and more dramatic situation. Although now and again he wins a point, the tide continues to sweep him toward disaster, and the tide is strong. Finally, there comes that time which fiction writers call the Black Moment. This is a point in the story at which it appears certain that the hero cannot possibly win. All hope is gone.

Since the reader is in sympathy with the hero—perhaps actually fond of him—this is an unpleasant moment. The reader, even though he fully appreciates the situation, still wants the hero to win. As he reads the story, the reader is actually in the battle, helping the hero to win.

Now comes the final battle. This is the crisis with all that it suggests. Here the hero puts all he has into the

struggle. Manfully he opposes all the forces against him
—forces as strong (or perhaps even stronger) as he. This
is It. This is the Battle of the Century. All is at stake.
The hero—being all hero—puts into the fight every last
ounce of strength at his command. He exerts himself as
never before. He utilizes extreme intelligence in this fight,
and, from some source, he gains such strength as you never
suspected anyone might possess. He fights and fights and
fights!

The antagonist, fully aware of the importance of this
battle, fights, too. Also, he calls in reserves of some kind.
He is not above using any kind of hold to win. He does
this. He fights a "dirty" fight.

This infuriates the hero. He puts forth even more effort
than before. He gives all of his strength in a terrific burst
of fury. *And he wins!*

This is the climax. This is the highest point of interest
in the story. It is near the end—perhaps within a few
paragraphs of the end of the story.

Now comes the reaction, the emotional relief the reader
feels. He is happy, indeed thrilled, to see this hero, who
so richly deserves the best and had every opportunity of
getting only the worst, emerge as victor. The reader is
delighted.

The article, to a considerable degree, follows the same
plan as that of the fiction story. This does not mean that
there must always be a hero to do battle. Instead, it may
be that the writer merely has a bit of information to give
to the reader. He wishes to make his offering as interesting
as possible. Therefore, he arranges his data in such an
order as to achieve the effect he desires.

ARTICLE ENDINGS

There still remains a major hurdle for you to clear before you offer your manuscript to an editor. It is difficult to exaggerate the importance of this portion of your article—the ending. Often it is only the final paragraph—perhaps fifty or seventy-five words. But what words! When you thoroughly understand its component parts and are able to execute them well, you will have come a long way toward the ranks of the professional writer.

What, then, are the components of the ending of a magazine article?

There are three: 1) A new, pertinent, and interesting fact; 2) material which will give a definite finality to the article; and 3) a statement, set of facts, or incident which will give the reader a feeling of complete satisfaction.

The ending of the article corresponds to the ending of the fiction story. As the fiction story leaves the reader with a feeling of satisfaction, of inevitability, so should the ending of the magazine article.

This means that it is not enough simply to conclude your article with a final period. That is for amateurs. You are going to reward your reader. You are going to make him glad he read your article. This is not a difficult procedure once you clearly understand the purpose of the article ending.

Suppose we need an ending for an article on karting. We might write:

Out of this invention has grown a new sport that is taking the country by storm. You may see karts all over the United States. Men and women, boys and girls, are getting fun out of speeding these miniature automobiles over small race tracks everywhere. All because a couple of boys set out to have a bit of fun for themselves.

This is a weak, unprofessional ending. The most you can say for it is that there is a final period at the end of the last sentence. That is hardly a compliment.

How can we improve this ending? By adding to it a new and pertinent fact, giving it a definite finality, and getting into it something that will give the reader a feeling of satisfaction—a reward for having read the article. Here is one way to do it:

This, then, is a thumbnail sketch of karting—America's newest sport. It appeals to persons of all ages. Father and son teams are the rule rather than the exception. Frequently mothers and daughters participate. Inexpensive, thrilling, and safe—there is seldom a serious injury resulting from karting—it is the ideal family sport.

And there is always the lure of winning. The lure is real. Only two years ago Jim Yamane was an amateur in karting. But today—with $1,500 prize money from Nassau—he is the World Karting Champion.

Who will win that title next year? And the next? The driver who produces the fastest kart and handles it most skillfully. There is real challenge, for that driver could be you.

Let us try another example. Suppose we are writing the end to an article about Harpers Ferry. In this article, after we have reported the dramatic events surrounding the John Brown insurrection, how do we write the ending?

Here is one possible way to do it:

Harpers Ferry, in 1859, was little more than a wide place in the road. But today it is attracting tourists by the thousands. Here you may walk where John Brown and his men walked, see the B & O bridge which they seized, and enter the John Brown fort in which Brown and his men were captured. It is a spot well worth a visit.

This is no ending at all. It fails on every count, and therefore we must reject it and in its stead write:

It is hardly a stretch of the imagination to state that the John Brown insurrection lighted the fuse which set off the Civil War.

More, Harpers Ferry, because of its strategic location at the junction of the Potomac and Shenandoah Rivers, was a key objective for the armies of both the North and South. One army tore it from the other repeatedly—a total of 9 times— during the War. Over a seemingly interminable period of time, Harpers Ferry was a virtual No Man's Land.

This, then, is the highly dramatic story of Harpers Ferry. Small wonder that it attracts increasing millions of visitors. It is, beyond all doubt, the scene of one of the most fantastic episodes in all American history.

This is an example of an engineered ending for this article. It contains not only one new and pertinent fact, but several facts of importance written forcefully. This ending has definite finality which well rewards the reader for his time and effort in perusing the article.

Your job, then, in writing the final part of your article, is to provide in compact language a new, pertinent, and intriguing fact; a definite finality to the article; and material which will well reward the reader for his time and effort in reading what you have written. When you have done that, you may rest assured that you have produced a professional ending for your offering. And that is a powerful selling point.

THE MARKED HIGHWAY

Here, then, is the checklist for you to use in your article writing. Make sure that each of your manuscripts has the following before you submit it to a magazine editor:

1. An alluring title
2. A compelling lead
3. Several professionally written anecdotes
4. A forceful climax
5. A completely satisfying end

These are signs along the highway to successful writing. Following them will require a bit of time and effort—say an extra five percent. But that five percent is important. It marks the line between the amateur and professional. It can mean the difference between abject failure and exhilarating success.

Chapter X

THE SELF-HELP ARTICLE

PERHAPS the most popular article you can write is the self-help piece. Some publications devote practically their entire contents to this kind of article.

A self-help article has one primary purpose: To aid the reader in some respect. It may help him to buy wisely, save money, advance in his business or profession, become a happier person, or to improve his lot in any one of a thousand respects.

One such article points out that everyone, at times, is lonely. Then the author suggests a means of combating this undesirable state. "Perhaps," he says in effect, "the best way to rout loneliness is to stop being self-centered and to give yourself to others."

In another article actress Helen Hayes quotes her mother as saying, "Helen, the most important thing in life is the knowledge that you have studied and worked hard and done the very best that is in you. That's achievement. Success is being praised by others, and that's nice, too. But it is not as important or satisfying as the inner knowledge that you have done your best. Always aim for achievement and forget about success."

This is a self-help article—one with profound meaning.

It is certain to help all who apply it to their lives. Articles such as those illustrated above are truly significant. They find a ready market.

SOURCE OF MATERIAL

Where do you get material for such articles?

You get it from your personal knowledge, from talking with others, from research. For instance: It well may be that you, as a housewife, have learned to handle household finances wisely. The information you have obtained very well might be of considerable aid to thousands—if not millions—of young housewives who have not yet learned the things you have discovered on this important subject.

Or, if you are employed in a personnel office, you may have acquired special information on how to make an application for a position. All too often it isn't the best qualified person who obtains the job. The successful applicant is the one who has learned how to make the best use of his abilities, how to prepare the application, how to dress, how to handle the interview. Competent instruction on these points would be of immense use to countless people.

Yet another example: As one who has suffered a bereavement, you may have received letters intended to console you but which actually intensified your suffering. If so, you may be in a position to help others write more appropriate letters of condolence. That article, too, would find a ready market.

And so it goes. No matter what your education, background, or life history, you have tucked away in your mind many bits of specific information which would help others in some manner. All of this is your personal material for self-help articles. Editors will pay you hand-somely for truly helpful articles of this kind.

IDEAS FOR SELF-HELP ARTICLES

As you examine your fund of knowledge, you may discover that you have many ideas suitable for self-help articles. This poses the question of which one is the most marketable. Here are a few suggestions to help you evaluate an idea for a self-help article:

1. Select an idea which appeals to a large group of people. The more individuals who would be interested in the article, other elements being equal, the better the idea.

2. Consider the appeal of your idea to the particular audience which comprises the readership of your prospective market. This means that you must learn something of the readers whom you hope to help. Who are they? What is their background? Why do they read this publication? What do they hope to gain from it? Would your idea actually help them? How much?

3. Is your article idea entirely sound in thought? If it contains any element of fakery, discard it.

4. Is this idea new to your readers? This need not be something of which the reader has never heard—only a new application, a new angle. But, in writing the article, see that you hew closely to the line. That is, give the reader the new angle, not the material that is "old hat."

5. Is the help your article would give well worth the reader's time? This is the final, irrevocable test for your article: Does it actually help the reader for whom it is intended?

6. Does your idea involve a technical subject? If so,

avoid it unless you have special knowledge in this field or can get an expert to help you with the project.

7. Does your idea lend itself to the production of an article which will make the project appear to be both relatively easy to complete and intriguing? It should.

8. If this is a construction piece, are sharp, step-by-step photographs available of the activity you describe? If not, you may do well to discard this idea in favor of another.

9. Does this idea lend itself to an alluring lead? This must not be fiction but it must be such that it will entice the reader to peruse the article. (Much, it is recognized, will depend upon how expertly you write the article.)

10. Is this idea one which you can present in a clear, moving manner or is it likely to bog down with details as the article unfolds? You will do well to avoid subjects which require long, tedious explanations.

11. What of the length of the article? Your self-help piece should be one which can be presented in 2,500 words —or even in shorter space. As a beginner, in particular, you should not undertake long, involved bits of writing.

12. What of the impact of your idea? Is it such that one, upon reading the finished article, would feel that he should follow the suggestions you outline? The best articles are those from which the reader feels that he can profit materially by accepting the plan of procedure which the article outlines.

MARKETS

Who will buy self-help articles?

Editors of juvenile publications, religious journals, house organs, trade publications, and general periodicals are all interested in articles that will help their readers.

If you put real help into your articles—help for a particular group of people—and offer the manuscript to the editor of a magazine for that group of readers, you will find a welcome mat ready and waiting for you. The prices are good and the demand is steady.

There can be no doubt but what you have much information that would be of considerable value to others. Examine it carefully. It can become your genuine bonanza.

As a writer of self-help articles, you face the eternal problem of producing exactly what a given magazine editor wants to buy. The best way to acquire this important bit of information is by analyzing what the editor in question has published. This means that you must study his publication.

In this chapter we shall examine how to go about the job of writing self-help articles for two types of magazines: religious magazines and trade journals.

RELIGIOUS MAGAZINES

If you wish to sell articles to this group of publications, you must learn definitely what they wish to publish. *Home Life,* a Christian family magazine, in a leaflet for writers outlines its editorial needs. "In general," says the editor "our articles must be Christian in tone, be related to family life, contain human interest, and be of high quality.

"*Home Life* is a contemporary picture of the best features of home life as it is lived today. It issues from the warp and woof of current home living. Fresh, human, pulsating, real life as it is lived, and as it should be lived —that is the sort of copy we want for *Home Life* . . ."

And, in order to give the full story, here is an article from *Home Life:*

WE HELPED OUR SON GO TO COLLEGE *

By Winfred Ernest Blevins

When our son Bill, then a junior in high school, came home one evening talking excitedly about his plans to go to college, my wife turned to me with a questioning look. It was clear she was bothered by the same question in my mind—"Where is the money coming from?"

Well, it does take money to keep a son in college. But any parent who really wants to can do so today, even on a meager salary.

We made this startling but pleasant discovery as we set out, not too hopefully at first, to make Bill's dream of a college education a reality. We checked with college admission offices, educational consultants and financial experts, college students, and parents with children in college before making our decision, but now we are confident we made the right one.

Sending a youngster to college may call for a closer budget at home and extra work by the student, but it can be done. Cooperation by the whole family will make the undertaking easier for everyone.

There are millions of dollars in college scholarships and millions more in loan funds available every year to worthy applicants. In addition, careful planning can cut big chunks out of college living expenses.

There are many colleges where students can earn while they learn. And there are insurance plans that enable parents to build up a college fund over a long period before the student enrolls.

First, let's take a look at what a college education costs these days so we can get an idea how much a child will need to go to college.

* From *Home Life,* Copyright © by the Sunday School Board of the Southern Baptist Convention, Nashville, Tennessee. Used by permission.

Right off we run into bad news. College costs are going up. And they are likely to keep going up. Col. Clarence Lovejoy, author of an excellent guide to U. S. colleges, says: "By 1970 we are going to have a total enrollment of five million students; and we'll be lucky if there are ten additional colleges, because building costs are prohibitive.

"So there will be a seller's market. Parents will be fighting to get their youngsters into school, and money will be no object."

Your son or daughter can go to college today for as little as $800 a year in some small but good college—even less if he lives at home. But he can spend $3,000 a year or more in some of the big schools. If there is an average, it would be about $1,000 to $1,200 per school year in Baptist senior colleges and state universities, somewhat less in junior colleges, but from $1,300 to $1,800 in most private colleges.

Remember that every college, no matter what its fees, loses money on every student. Private institutions depend on grants and gifts to support them, while public schools depend on taxes. In either school there are scholarships for applicants who can meet the qualifications.

A mother I spoke to about a scholarship for her daughter got a faraway look in her eye. "I suppose my daughter will never be the intellectual type," she said, "so she can't get a scholarship."

The mother was wrong. Scholarships, we found out, are probably the most used of major ways to finance a child's education.

According to the U.S. Department of Health, Education and Welfare, there are 237,370 scholarships worth $65,736,950 available every year to college students. They pay (in part) tuition, room, board, and special fees. They are awarded by colleges, business and industry, public foundations, civic and charitable groups, public spirited individuals, and by churches and church groups, including some Baptist conventions. The amount of scholarship money and the number of awards available stagger the imagination.

Because parents and college students generally do not know about these scholarships, many go begging each year. They make it possible, however, for worthy students to overcome financial obstacles in their path to a college education.

Academic achievement is essential to win a scholarship, but the applicant does not have to be a genius. In most cases, need is the determining factor. A brilliant youngster from a wealthy family is less likely to receive a scholarship than a student from a low-income family whose grades are not so impressive.

Most colleges have some funds for worthy students. Scholarships generally range from $25 to $1,500. An alert parent whose child needs financial assistance to attend college should investigate several possible sources of aid. A loan, scholarship, part-time work, or a combination of these will make it possible for almost any youngster willing to work for it to get his college education.

The place to start in organizing a program of this type is to study catalogs and make inquiries at the college as to the kind of assistance available and the requirements. Be prepared to supply evidence that financial need exists.

If your child fails to win a scholarship, he can always get by on self-help. This is just a new word for working his way through college. More than 60 per cent of all college students do some work to defray expenses. It is estimated that at least $120,000,000 is earned every year by college students. An A student can handle as much as thirty hours of work per week, it is believed, and still keep up his studies. Students whose average grade is no better than a C should not take on more than twelve hours per week.

Part-time work will not hurt any youngster or his social opportunities. College authorities agree that part-time work is a very healthy and useful experience that helps provide a smooth transition from school to business or industry.

There's certainly nothing wrong or degrading in working one's way through college. Herbert Hoover worked while he was a student at Stanford University. Thousands of other students have worked to pay expenses. Information relating to part-time work for students at almost any school is available on the campus.

Though scholarships and self-help constitute the largest source of aid to college students, there are other ways. A college loan fund, for example, is convenient and useful.

Our son chose a combination of plans. After we studied the catalogs of most of the Midwestern colleges, he decided to get a job for that summer. With the money he could make through the summer, he could pay his tuition and in addition he would try for a scholarship.

Meanwhile, he and I arranged a loan just in case his efforts for a scholarship failed. He did that because the first year, we thought, is most important, and the fewer worries and distractions he had to keep him from his books, the better. With the matter of financing settled, the problem of choosing a college was before us.

Not long ago children went to the college their parents chose for them. Some families attended the same college for generations, and for a child to even want to go elsewhere seemed disloyal.

Today the picture has changed. Children like to make their own choices, and most parents realize that guiding a child is better than trying to dominate him. With this in mind, we tried to help our son choose his college. Believe me, it is no easy task.

There are two principal types of institutions, the college and the university. A college, broadly speaking, is smaller than a university. It is a single unit, while a university is composed of a number of colleges and schools.

The college has a distinct educational policy of its own and is centrally administrated. In a university, each college and school is a self-contained unit. Policies in its different schools and colleges are not necessarily unified. To be sure, there are uniform rules which each college and school in a university must observe, but, by and large, policies of the various colleges vary widely.

There are approximately two thousand institutions of higher learning in this country. In that group, we knew, were colleges in which our son could get the kind of education he wanted and could get it in the kind of atmosphere he wanted to study in.

We thought it important to visit some colleges. On week ends we drove to several, looked into the buildings, talked to members of the faculty and the admissions staffs. We had lunch in dining rooms and chatted with students. We made notes on everything that we thought might enter into our son's final decision.

Probably no college is ever selected for any single reason. Parents usually favor a college close to home. This saves time and money in traveling to and from school, making it easy to come home for Thanksgiving, Christmas, and at the end of the semester.

The academic rating of colleges should also be given consideration. If there is any doubt about a school's rating, check to see if it is accredited by the regional accrediting agency. This information usually is available at any public library. We wrote several letters to universities making inquiry about certain colleges, but the general requirements are usually listed in the catalog. Our attention, for the most part, was focused on our son's specific needs.

For example, Bill was very active in our church. He was a

member of the Sunday school, president of the young people's Training Union, Junior RA counselor, and a member of the choir. Church work was a good part of his life.

Adjustments that our son would surely have to make—staying away from home for long periods, making new friends, learning to live with other people—were enough without requiring him to adjust to life without his church. Naturally, we looked for a college with a Christian atmosphere, in a town where there were Baptist churches.

Finally our son's list of colleges was narrowed to three. We visited these colleges again and noted, among other things, the religious spirit on each campus. It was then that our son chose Hannibal-LaGrange College, a Southern Baptist school at Hannibal, Missouri. Not that Hannibal-LaGrange is the best college in the United States, but it is one where our son could take the subjects he wanted and take Christ with him.

Perhaps no consideration is more important than the spiritual tone of the college selected. Impressions and choices made during college years often last a lifetime.

Since Bill entered college, he has told us that he is very happy in his work. We are happy too, because we had a small part in helping him make his choice. The corners of our budget that had to be cut to help him were trimmed with pleasure. We consider his education a family affair. It is a joint undertaking—parents and child.

In most families sacrifices are necessary when a child goes to college. Financial burdens are substantial when children are in high school, and the additional costs of college can make the load staggering.

But we have found that this is only the beginning. We have had to re-educate ourselves. Our son not only has made us proud of him, but he has brought new education into our home.

College training was cut short for my wife and me, but we

have to hold our own at the dinner table when Bill comes home. We've had to do a lot of cramming to get ourselves up-to-date about humanities, social science, communications, the natural sciences, psychology, electronics. This has been the hardest part, but we've enjoyed it.

Analysis

The purpose of this article is to show how a family with limited funds can send a child through college. To that end the writer offered the following suggestions:

1. Conduct an investigation before making up your mind as to what college or university to attend. This investigation will include talking with the personnel in the admissions offices, educational consultants, financial experts, students in the college, faculty members, and parents of the students.

2. Insist that the whole family cooperate in this project. This will make the task easier for all concerned.

3. Look into the possibility of getting a scholarship.

4. Get a definite idea of what the cost of a college education is likely to be.

5. Find out if the college you are considering has a fund available for worthy students in need.

6. Learn what opportunities to earn money a student might have in a given college.

7. Remember the possibility of summer employment as a means of helping to pay the college bills.

8. Compare the academic ratings of various colleges and universities which you seriously consider.

9. Make sure the college atmosphere is thoroughly Christian.

10. Consider the courses the college or university has to

offer, its position in the academic world, and the particular qualifications it has to give you the education you desire for your child.

Comment

In view of all this information, is it any wonder to you that *Home Life,* a Christian family magazine, bought and paid good money for this article? Wouldn't you have bought it, had you been editor?

And, finally, the article sold because it offered real help to its readers who, although unable financially to send their children through college, actually want them to have the advantage of a college education. That kind of help will regularly sell articles to magazines of this kind.

TRADE JOURNALS

Trade journals are fairly bulging with self-help articles. Among these magazines is *Motor* magazine, a well-edited monthly. One of the leading periodicals in its field, it is designed to help people engaged one way or another in the automotive business. And the more help a given article contains, the more down-to-earth practical ideas which others can use, the more suitable it is for *Motor.*

This periodical goes to automobile dealers, car salesmen, garagemen, service managers, and service station operators—people who must keep abreast of every phase of the business. Thus, market tips report that *Motor* wants outstanding merchandising, sales, and management articles which contain ideas that can be adapted to other similar operations.

In this magazine you will find such titles as:

"Ball Joint Replacement Can Be Easier"

"Pinpoint Causes of Mysterious Misses"

"Fast Repair of Damaged Front End"
"Build Your Own Imported Car Service Business"
"Get Your Share of Summer TBA Sales"
"Don't Take 'I'll Be Back' as an Answer"

The best way, of course, to understand what *Motor* uses is to study one of the articles it has published. Here is a typical example:

DON'T TAKE "I'LL BE BACK" AS AN ANSWER *

By Harlan A. Klepfer

Recently I was approached by a salesman who said, "All I ever hear is hot air about selling. Do this, do that, rules and more rules, but no one ever tells me how to *close a sale* and get the customer to *sign* on the dotted line."

He went on to say how discouraged he gets when prospects walk out saying, "Well, I don't think I will do anything right now. Thank you, I'll be back." A few days pass, sometimes a week, and this prospect is contacted by phone and the salesman gets the final blow. His prospect has signed an order somewhere else.

It certainly is discouraging, there is no doubt about it.

Let us look into this problem of closing a prospect. First of all, there are some customers who, for reasons beyond your control, you will *not* be able to close. Those reasons could be: The price policy of the house, an over-supply of that year and model used car, the customer is already well satisfied with his present dealer and is just checking the market with a closed mind or the customer finds he just can't afford a newer car now. These and possibly other situations are pretty much beyond your control and you just have to learn to skip over these

* Reprinted from *Motor* magazine, Copyright © 1960, The Hearst Corporation.

situations and start on the next customer, who is bound to be better.

If, however, these prospects are *buyers* and they walk out on you with those famous words, "I'll be back," they obviously were *not convinced* that they should have bought the product from you *or* they were not in a position to sign at that moment regardless of what you did. Let us examine these two types.

To get a better picture of the problem of the man who is not convinced about the product, take an obviously poor example of an effort to close a customer. This salesman rushes up to a prospect who has just walked into the salesroom and says, "For some money you can have what I am selling, if you sign this order now."

He did some things right: He approached the customer and asked for an order. Fine, but this bewildered customer doesn't even know what it is that he can buy, whether or not it's any good or if he can use it. Furthermore, he has no idea of the price and knows nothing of the person from whom he is to make the purchase. Why should this customer "close a deal"?

Now, in contrast, here is another salesman. He greets the customer promptly, introduces himself, talks in a friendly manner and shows his product with enthusiasm. He gets the prospect to talk about his problems and needs while he listens with a sincere interest. Then he gives his best advice in recommending which product the customer should buy, a product which will be of the greatest benefit to the customer.

This salesman has his customer participate in the planned demonstration of the various features of the product, then quotes a fair price that leaves a profit for the house. He figures monthly payments accurately and asks the customer to sign an order. If the customer does not accept the proposition and starts to hedge, the salesman asks more questions to find the *real objections* (which are not always money) and comes up with a reasonable solution to the objections.

Then he tactfully again asks for the order in a different way.

He is prepared to write the order completely, take a deposition, arrange for any transfer of insurance, financing, preparation of all papers and a smooth final delivery of his product.

"There you go back on that 'selling kick' again," I can just hear you say. "Get back to the point, how do *I* close a car deal?"

All right, let's get back to closing a car deal. Just where in the second presentation would the salesman close the deal? At the end when the customer signs? Yes, but he *really* started to close the sale at the very beginning when he first greeted the customer. Everything he did and said from that moment on was making it easier for the customer to justify to himself, and to others, his purchase of the car.

Compare this with the man who said, "For some money you can have what I am selling if you sign this order blank now." One asks for the sale but gives *no reason why* the customer should buy, while the other salesman gives one solid reason after the other, all based on facts that are tailored to the customer's interests and problems.

There is no doubt about which man has the easier job closing the sale. The second man set out to convince the prospect that he should buy his product, giving reasons and overcoming objections. Then when he asked the prospect to sign the order he was less likely to get that famous farewell phrase, "Thank you, not now. I'll be back."

The other problem is the man whom you have convinced about the product but who is not in a position to sign an order at the moment. When the customer says "no" the first time, the salesman should, by asking questions, find out if his prospect *can* sign right there and then. This takes a little "fishing" and the ability to have the customer take you into his confidence because hidden behind the "I want to think it over" could be many reasons, any one of which would make it *impossible* for you to get a signed order at that time.

Some of these reasons could be: "I'd better talk this over

with my wife first," "I like the car but I didn't really think it was going to cost so much," "I had better check my bank balance before I sign up," "I think I can get the money through the Credit Union at a lower rate," "I wonder if my brother-in-law can get me a better deal?" "Bertha told me not to sign anything," or "The kid at the gas station said he wanted my old car. I wonder how much he will pay?"

Those and many more are "hidden objections" that will put off closing a deal unless you take the time to ask questions and smoke out the real obstacles to signing the order. Unless you can get through to these and work out a satisfactory solution you are just "spinning your wheels" while the prospect inches toward the door.

What are we going to do with this type? Well, let us see. When you feel that your prospect has a definite interest and seems to be sold on the product but asks for a "little time," try to find out *why*. If you can't get through to the *real reason* or if he objects to your jumping into the demonstrator with him and going home *at once* to talk to Bertha, you do not have much choice but to let him "walk." However, when you are planning your work sheet for the *next day*, put him down as a hot prospect who must be contacted. Other than appointments you have already made this man should be your number one objective for the day.

As a rule, a person thinking about buying a car will talk about it at home for a while, comment on the new models as he is out driving with the family, discuss cars with the fellows at work, then finally he is moved to action such as visiting a dealer or calling his favorite salesman on the phone to ask a "few questions."

Then you have to work fast because if he is fairly certain of the product and he has already "talked to Bertha," something will happen in about 48 hours. If you are at the right place at this "right time," which is your business, you will have a very good chance to close him. If he cools off, it is a hard job (and usually costs more money) to get the prospect "worked up" again.

As in any sport, the right timing is all important, so the right timing is *vital* to closing a deal. You must get the "feel" of your prospect and know when to push for a close. It might be during the demonstration, back in the closing room or in his living room with his wife that evening but you must "strike while the iron is hot."

Another important factor in closing that cannot be overlooked is *money*. After everything else has been done, pointed out, demonstrated and discussed, last, but not least, comes a basic problem of money. If enough desire has been created during the sales presentation, the money part might be slightly minimized but never completely eliminated.

Figure the deal carefully yourself first. Check your figures, then present them with confidence to your prospect, making him feel that he is really lucky that he came to you and this just happens to be a special occasion that allows you to give him such an attractive proposition.

Be able to justify your figures and argue your position with facts if necessary. If there is a question, be able to show used car values, figure his cost per year, show that he is paying "a little more" because this is a different model or point out the generous allowance he is receiving for his old car. Don't let him tie you up at this point, keep up your pace and keep going.

If you sense a lack of agreement between the husband and wife, sometimes it helps to excuse yourself to "double check the price" or "see if there is a certain color in stock" or some other reason just to give the couple a chance to talk in private. Then when you return in a few minutes you will find they are in agreement and you can continue closing the sale.

Keep in mind when you figure each deal that the house must make a profit that will more than just cover expenses if you intend to be on the payroll very long. That is most important. Also, add in a little "extra" because it is a very comfortable feeling to have a little room to compromise should the customer say: "All right, knock off that $25 and I'll sign right now."

Try to avoid closing all your deals with a money compromise because once you start, it becomes a habit that often is not necessary. Also, your customers will remember you as an "easy chisel" and the next time you are trying to close them, they will expect the same tactics and probably ask for *more* than the last time. It becomes a one-way road that is difficult to back up on and also brings down the quality of your product and your selling.

Another type of money situation that could end in a compromise close starts with a ridiculous "flat offer" on a take it or leave it basis or "beat this deal" and I'll sign.

Don't panic at this. In fact, often this is a pretty good sign. It means you have sold the product all right, you are talking to the right person because he is able to sign the order and the timing is good, too. At least he is alive. Stop right there and figure out his proposition, either in your head or on a piece of paper. If you know your position was real close to start with, stop in horror *at once* at the thought of taking anything less or if he is not too far off with his offer, let him know you are considering it as you refigure and perhaps suggest a compromise.

In any event, you know the cost of the car you are selling and you know the true value of his used car. The difference is simple arithmetic. Don't let a complete novice throw you off your stride by trying to tell you that 2 plus 2 equals 6 when you know better. Tell him, "Oh, no!" Back off and work around again. This takes time, but you certainly can't put your time to better use than working to close with a prospect that is so close to buying.

Another approach that is often effective in closing a sale is to call the manager into the closing room. This gives added force to your statements, immediate approval of your deal or someone to arbitrate any problems you may have encountered. However, you must be sure that he understands what your position is and what the exact problem is because it is very difficult to walk into a closing room and pick up the tempo of an hour's selling without knowing just what has transpired.

Also, be very sure, when you call in the manager, that you have left him some room to "move a little" or you have really put your boss in a tough spot.

So, in answer to the question, "How can *I* close more deals?" I would say the secret to a higher percentage of closed sales is a complete and convincing presentation of the *right product* to the *right party* at the *right time* for the *right price*. If any of these four elements is not right, your job becomes infinitely harder and your percentage of closed sales falls off.

Analysis

If you will look at this article from the editor's chair, you may discover that the writer gave a considerable amount of practical help in this short bit of interesting prose. For instance, he:

1. Deals with a problem of vital interest to *Motor* readers.

2. Offers specific help in the way of analysis. Only by learning precisely why a customer objects to your offer can you intelligently cope with the situation.

3. Declares that, from the first approach to a customer, the salesman must build confidence. This is a tremendously potent sales factor.

4. Shows a method of dealing with a prospect who, although convinced, still refuses to sign a contract.

5. Makes it appear relatively simple to close a sale. This helps to build salesman self-confidence.

6. Offers numerous practical suggestions which may enable the salesman to compromise a bit yet close a profitable deal.

7. Offers personal suggestions of value to the salesman —his attitude, tact, objective.

8. Avoids deadwood. The article is written without padding and all of it is pertinent to the point of the article.

9. Keeps the article moving. There is nothing static about it. It is a readable piece of prose.

10. Ends the article on a constructive note.

Comment

Now look at this article from the salesman's point of view. You will see that each of the foregoing elements will be of actual help to him in one of the most difficult aspects of his job—closing the sale.

This article, then, gives the reader something. It helps him become a better salesman. It aids him to make more money for himself and for his company. This is extremely practical. In view of these facts, it is small wonder that *Motor* found this article acceptable. The editor knew it would actually help thousands of his readers. That's why he bought it.

Fundamental Technique

Your job, as the author of a self-help article, is to give your readers real assistance. You can do this only by imparting information that is new to them and practical. This gives you two significant guidelines, i.e.:

1. Narrow your article to one subject. This is necessary because of space limitations. Winfred Ernest Blevins did this by showing how he and his wife helped their son go to college. The Blevins article deals exclusively with this one subject.

In our other example, written by Harlan A. Klepfer, the author is even more sharply in focus. Here the subject is just one aspect of salesmanship—*how to close a sale*. Klepfer considers this problem from many angles but never gets away from that subject.

Here, then, is a big lesson for you: Select one subject for your self-help article and in that article confine yourself exclusively to that subject.

2. See that the information you offer is practical. You obtain such data by what is called depth research. This simply means that you must explore your one subject in detail. You read the newest data in the field of your research, interview experts, and apply your own intellect to the problem.

From all of these sources, you produce solutions which others are using successfully. Perhaps you may come up with a new idea or two of your own that has real merit. Helen Hayes certainly did that in the article in which she quoted her mother as saying that success is not as important as achievement—the knowledge that you have worked hard and done the very best that's in you.

You can do this, too. You will do it if you persist in depth research. That is the only way to obtain practical information for your self-help articles.

When you have achieved that end, your job is all but done. You need have no fear for the outcome of your article. There will be no selling problem. Editors will learn that you have mastered a tremendously important aspect of writing. They will vie with each other to publish your work. That is both achievement and success. It gives you a mighty fine feeling.

Chapter XI

THE TRAVEL ARTICLE

ALTHOUGH NO one can predict accurately what even a few months may bring, the present trends indicate that for many years there will be a strong demand for the travel article. If you wish to try writing travel articles, learn to write them well.

The travel article is a self-help piece for travelers. It may deal with the safety factor in automobile travel; suggest ways and means of conserving time, energy, and money while on a trip; give practical suggestions for making the trip more delightful; report intriguing facts about a particular place or series of places, an object or a series of objects. The total effect of a well-executed travel article is to encourage travel.

Besides encouraging travel, the travel article offers a satisfying substitute for travel, giving the "you-are-there" feeling to those who cannot and may never travel but get vicarious pleasure from reading vividly written articles about faraway places.

How will you know whether the travel article you have written is good enough to make an editor feel his readers would profit from reading it?

There are two answers to this: First, send it to an editor and let him tell you. This is the easy—and more unsatisfactory—way. The other method is to compare what you have written with articles published in the magazine which you think might buy your story.

How do you compare them? Place your article beside the published one. Analyze these articles objectively, point by point: the beginning, body, end, composition, new information, lure. Just what new information do you have to offer? How fascinating is it? Have you written forcefully? Does the article really make the reader want to see the spot you describe?

Does your article grow in interest as it advances? It should. Is there a real—not a phony—climax?

Now try to imagine you are a reader, not the author of this sterling piece of scintillating prose. Begin reading it as critically as if another had written it. Then ask yourself the Big Question: Would I read and find this profitable if another had written it?

If you can honestly answer that question in the affirmative, you may fairly conclude that your article is probably salable.

MARKETS

Among the small magazines there is a remarkable similarity of requirements for the travel article. Therefore, your problem is not one of preparing a story to fit a given magazine—or even a type of magazine. Instead, your main consideration must be to make certain that you provide genuine information and help to prospective travelers.

Almost without exception we feel that our vacation periods are too short. Consequently, we welcome suggestions which enable us to save time while we travel. One answer to the perennial question of how to save time while traveling is found in the following article which was published in *Dodge News*.

FOR A SUPER VACATION
TAKE A SUPERHIGHWAY *

By Len Barnes

If you haven't taken a long motor vacation trip in the past few years, you'll be amazed at how much faster you can get where you're going this summer.

Joseph Schuler of Milwaukee, for instance, decided to visit his parents in northern Maine this spring. Not having made the trip by auto in 10 years, he figured it would take 31 hours to drive there. Schuler was surprised to make it in 20 hours. He used turnpikes and divided highways almost exclusively from his front door to his destination.

Schuler began his trip on one of the four important roads opened since last summer, the Illinois Tollway, a 187-mile affair which vaults over the Chicago-area traffic. Heading out of Chicago, he picked up the Calumet Skyway, hooked onto the Indiana, Ohio, Pennsylvania, and New Jersey Turnpikes, New York and Connecticut Parkways and Massachusetts Turnpikes.

Schuler did not see a stop light or encounter any cross traffic or trains. He averaged 50 miles per hour, as compared to a 35-mile-per-hour rate on average highways.

Between Chicago and New York City now stretches the longest four-lane divided highway in the world—900 miles.

You may be able to save as much as 20 per cent of last year's driving time during this year's vacation—or increase your vacation horizon by 1,000 miles—by routing yourself over some of the 10,000 miles of toll turnpikes and four-lane, divided freeways which will be in use this summer. They have

---

* Reprinted through the courtesy of *Dodge News Magazine*, published by the Dodge Division of Chrysler Corporation.

brought every place in the United States within driving range if you have three weeks' time.

We are now in the midst of the world's greatest highway-building program, which by the mid-1970's will bring 41,000 miles of super-roads into the National System of Interstate Highways. Almost any place you choose to drive, you should pass near enough to one of these roads to utilize its speed and safety. More than 5,215 miles of this system are now in use.

Important freeways opened since last summer include two links to the New York Thruway: The New England Thruway, linking New York City and the Connecticut Turnpike; and the Berkshire section, vaulting the Hudson River and connecting with the Massachusetts Turnpike. Twenty miles of the Tulsa bypass complete the 225-mile expressway between Joplin, Mo., and Oklahoma City. California's Route 40 is an improved 122-mile section from Sacramento, California to Nevada.

You'll be able to tell which of the four-laners are on the Interstate System by the route markers. The markers are shield-shaped—red, white and blue—with the word "Interstate" on the top. Information and direction signs along these routes are billboard-size, with foot-high letters, white on reflectorized green for best day-night visibility, to alert you to interchanges, cities ahead, roadside rest, service and lodging.

There are some drivers who actually don't like these concrete and asphalt ribbons with no curve or hill of more than three degrees, with always at least 600 feet straightway ahead, and with 300-foot-wide right of way.

"As the number of miles of superhighway increases, we actually get more requests for non-super-routes," said one travel counselor. "People often choose the turnpike route in going to their destination and then ask for the 'byway' route returning, so they can get there in a hurry, then absorb the color of the area on the way back."

If you've been using the same old holiday route for 10 years, or if you're planning a different destination this year, it will pay you to check up. You can do this by visiting your local AAA Club or by writing to state tourist departments.

Analysis

A study of this article reveals that the author planned to aid the traveler by pointing out that:

1. One can safely average 50 miles an hour on a super-highway as compared with 35 miles an hour on the average road. This amounts to a real saving in time.

2. Superhighways have brought every place in the United States within driving range of one who has a three-week vacation. No matter where one wishes to go, he can probably use a superhighway at least part of the distance.

3. This year you may save as much as 20 per cent of last year's vacation time—and increase your vacation horizon by 1,000 miles—by routing yourself over superhighways. This really amounts to lengthening your vacation period.

4. Important freeways regularly being opened tend to make traffic safer even at high rates of speed. A big and continuing program is under way.

5. By using the superhighway in going to your destination, you actually have additional time to use as you wish.

Comment

In this article the author gave valid help to a travel problem common to almost everyone. Moreover, he stuck to one subject—saving time. He did not try to make this into a conglomerate article, one involving all phases of travel. He presented his material clearly and forcefully. And, as a result, he sold the article to an excellent market. By helping others, he helped himself to an editorial check. His plan will work for you, too. Try it!

UNBLAZED TRAILS

Another type of travel article tells the reader what to see when he travels. The editor of *Plymouth Traveler* suggests the "copy desert" as subject matter. The phrase "copy desert" is used to describe that part of the country that is off the beaten path. It is merely another way of saying, "Write about something new. Give the readers a different bill of fare; they've had enough of the old stand-bys."

Is there anything new under the sun? Yes! Have you heard of the Ox Gad Tree? Or Bellefourche, South Dakota? Or modern lancing tournaments? The chances are strong that you have heard of none of these—and more important, that your potential readers haven't either. Yet each place has a travel story in it—and perhaps several.

Your job as a writer of a "Things to See" travel article is to find and report fascinating facets of a place, a series of places, an object or a series of objects. If you choose material that is relatively new, your task will probably be infinitely easier than if you select subjects which have been published time and time again. What is even more important, you will find it far easier to sell the new than the old. For instance:

WASHINGTON'S FIRST MONUMENT *

The first monument to George Washington is all but hidden from the public. Tucked away on a rocky Maryland crag, it

* Reprinted by permission of *The Blade*.

is completely concealed until one is within a few rods of it, and it's inaccessible except by foot or on horseback.

Because of these facts only a handful of people, relatively speaking, have heard of it. Far fewer have seen it. Yet it is one of the most fascinating of our national memorials.

Constructed of Maryland "blue rock" it is 34 feet high, 20 feet in diameter and of solid stone except for the spiral stairway which winds through its center to the top.

Volunteer laborers built it. They assembled on the Boonsboro, Md., public square at 7 a.m., July 4, 1827—just 28 years after Washington's death—and marched behind the flag and a fife and drum corps to the summit of South Mountain, 1,500 feet above the village.

There these patriots set about constructing a monument to keep alive the memory of Washington. However, since no water supply was readily available, the volunteers carefully selected and accurately cut huge stones and laid them, without mortar, in a cylindrical design.

At noon the Reverend Clingham, a gentleman whose warm patriotism caused him to ignore "a constitution rendered infirm by age and bad health," dedicated the memorial.

By the end of the day the monument was 15 feet high, a substantial beginning of a memorial to the man who, under most adverse circumstances, had led the Colonial army to a final victory.

Memorials such as this are not built in a day. After the "busy season," the Boonsboro citizens returned to their ambitious project and completed it by fall.

"I am satisfied," wrote historian E. H. Pitcher, "of the correctness of the claim that the South Mountain edifice was the first to be dedicated to George Washington."

This is far from the complete story of the "South Mountain edifice." There's a sequel.

Before the monument was 50 years old, it had fallen into

ruins. Finally the Independent Order of Odd Fellows of Boonsboro sponsored its restoration.

On August 18, 1882, the Honorable William T. Hamilton, then governor of Maryland, speaking before several thousand people, dedicated the reconstructed memorial.

But even this was not to last. Faulty construction, a bolt of lightning and the ravages of time took their toll with the result that, for the second time within a century, the memorial was in ruins.

In 1935 the Maryland Department of Forestry and the National Park Service, in conjunction with the Civilian Conservation Corps, restored the memorial to its present condition. Its latest dedication—July 4, 1936—occurred just 109 years after the original service.

Analysis

1. This is a "desert copy" article. It reports something relatively few people know yet which is of considerable interest.

2. The article appears in a Washington's Birthday issue of the Toledo *Blade Sunday Supplement.*

3. The lead is calculated to arouse interest, to lure the reader on to reading the remainder of the article.

4. Paragraph two gives direction to the article. From the final sentence in that paragraph the reader knows that this article contains additional unusual and probably fascinating facts.

5. With paragraph three the writer begins to document his statement that this is one of our most fascinating memorials. He produces evidence to convince the reader that this statement is true.

6. The major portion of this article concerns the unusual facts of the memorial's construction, the ravages of

time, the rebuilding of it, and the fact that it was in ruins twice within a century.

7. By the final paragraph of the article, the reader learns that this is truly a remarkable memorial—one with three lives—and it still stands in good repair.

8. The article moves. It has directness, concise writing, and it advances to a satisfactory conclusion.

9. Perhaps the most outstanding feature of this article is the writing. It displays imagination which helps to make the piece readable. The first sentence is an excellent example.

10. Somehow the author managed to give the reader the feeling that he is actually seeing the memorial itself. This, of course, is an added appeal.

Comment

You can learn much from this article. First, in all probability near you there is a little known memorial, landmark, or spot notable in local, state, or national history. This very well may be a suitable subject for an article similar to "Washington's First Monument."

One market for such an article is your local Sunday Supplement. You will find the Sunday Supplements a friendly and worthwhile market.

Early in your article you must give it direction, and then you must see that it moves in the direction planned. If you can make your article timely, you will increase your chances of making a sale. And a few sharp black and white photographs with which to illustrate your article will also help.

The beginning writer, especially, can profit from writing articles for the Sunday Supplement market.

THE BEATEN TRAIL ARTICLE

Even if you do not have the opportunity to visit the "copy desert," you can produce "What to See" travel articles. You can write such articles about the Beaten Trail—Yellowstone National Park, Miami Beach, Washington, Hollywood, New York City—and sell them once you learn how to do it.

Here is the Beaten Trail formula: Give your reader something he has not heard before, something fascinating, something that will surprise him. How can one possibly do that with, let us say, Disneyland? Through research.

If you research a subject very carefully, you can find little-known, interesting material even on the Beaten Trail. You can make your articles more exciting than those of writers who have done a less thorough research job. This extra effort in research is what will help you sell your work.

You may ask what could be fascinating or unusual about a place so much on the Beaten Trail as Disneyland, for example. With careful research the author of the following article found new amazing facts which the reader did not possess. This made it worth publishing, and the author was able to sell it to *Dodge News Magazine* for a substantial amount.

AMERICA'S MOST FANTASTIC PLAYGROUND *

By Robert Rolopson, Jr.

During Disneyland's opening ceremonies in 1955, Walt Disney stated that his Magic Kingdom would never be com-

* Reprinted through the courtesy of *Dodge News Magazine*, published by the Dodge Division of Chrysler Corporation.

pleted. Since that time, more than 17 million visitors from all 50 states, and nearly every nation in the world, have spun its turnstiles. On opening day there were 22 attractions, exclusive of exhibits and shows. Five years and $12,600,000 later, there are 47.

This is America's most fantastic playground—a giant park that makes a child's heart sing and a Russian premier grumble (because they wouldn't let him *see* it). Located at Anaheim, Calif., 27 miles southeast of Los Angeles on the Santa Ana Freeway, it encompasses 160 acres, boasts 20 restaurants and "refreshment corners" and a 235-room hotel. But you can always count on something *new* being added to Disneyland.

Two summers ago, Uncle Walt's travels took him to Switzerland, and the result was Disneyland's 145-foot scale replica of the famous Matterhorn, complete with "snow", glacial grottoes, icicle caverns, waterfalls, live mountain climbers, and two thrilling bobsled runs.

The Matterhorn's 60 bobsleds are gravity-powered and guided by tracks of welded three-inch pipe, allowing the four-man sleds to safely climb, dip, bank around high speed curves and pass behind and across waterfalls. They spiral through the grottoes and outside the mountain where the riders can look down and glimpse the wonders of the park before racing to a halt in a "glacial" lake at the bottom.

The Swiss "skyway" cables still travel between *Fantasyland* and *Tomorrowland*, but the colorful little buckets now pass right through the center of the Matterhorn, where the passengers catch glimpses of bobsleds as they race through the ice caverns.

Very few citizens have the influence to take a cruise on a submarine, but visitors to Disneyland can now take an exciting, inexpensive dive beneath the waves in one of eight authentic, fully air-conditioned submarines. Designed from technical data furnished by General Dynamics Corporation (builders of America's nuclear subs), each 56-foot sub has individual seating and portholes for 38 passengers.

Propeller-driven, they follow an underwater guide rail "beneath the Seven Seas" to the legendary Lost Continent of Atlantis, where sunken treasure and huge statues are covered with 24 carat gold sparkle, and are guarded by a huge octopus.

The voyage continues past the "Graveyard of Sunken Ships", and under the "Polar Ice Cap" to re-create the historic voyage made by the U.S.S. *Nautilus*. The water is populated with hundreds of lifelike fish, which swim past the portholes of the sub. There are sharks, manta rays, moray eels, giant squid, fluorescent fish, barracuda, and lesser known denizens like exotic mermaids and an 80-foot sea serpent!

Perhaps the most significant of the new attractions is the Disneyland-Alweg monorail system. Two ultra-modern streamlined trains, each with a capacity of 82 passengers, carry an *average* of 100,000 persons a week.

Using Westinghouse 300-volt subway motors and running on rubber tires, the two three-car trains travel over a one mile concrete beam-way. This beam is supported by cement pylons reaching heights of 34 feet, and is substantially the same size and scale as those that would be used for any metropolitan single track system.

If the Disneyland trains were used in regular metropolitan transit, they would be capable of speeds in excess of 80 miles per hour. The basic design, including motive power, braking and safety systems, could be used, but would call for larger trains to accommodate baggage, mail and standing passenger space. Metropolitan officials from major cities in the United States have already inspected the system, with others scheduled to tour the park this fall.

The rubber-tire, concrete-beam system was originally developed by the Alweg Company, and has been under development and testing at Cologne, Germany for six years. The trains themselves were designed by Disney engineers, and are made of lightweight aluminum, plastic and stainless steel. It is interesting to note that all door and access panels are fastened with Dodge trunk lid latches!

This daily operating monorail is the first such scheduled system in the United States, and at the rate of 2,100 passengers per hour, may shortly make Walt Disney the king of the transportation world.

Disneyland's most popular form of transportation, the Autopia Freeway, has been expanded into four multi-level "Super Autopias" over which youngsters of all ages drive gasoline-powered sport cars. The colorful little cars are not on rails, depending instead on the driver's skill and 360-degree spring bumpers, which rebound against high curbings. However, the new freeway passes by the submarine pens, the Matterhorn, over the lagoons and whitewater rapids of the speedboat excursions, and under the monorail beams. All of which provide a parade of eye-filling distractions . . . requiring more than a little skill to drive the complete course without touching a curb!

Last, but not least of the "new" Disneyland, is *Circarama USA,* produced especially for the World's Fair in Brussels, and later shown at the U.S. Exhibit in Moscow. The film, utilizing 11 separate projectors and 11 screens to produce a 360-degree effect, is a fast-moving tour of the United States.

Of special interest to out-of-state visitors is the summer season schedule at Disneyland, which will feature a wide variety of special activities highlighted by the nighttime show. The "Fantasy of the Sky" features a major fireworks display, exploding a shower of color over the *Fantasyland* Castle and the Matterhorn (nightly at 9 o'clock, from June 11 through Sept. 11).

Disneyland begins its "Open Every Day" schedule May 25— from 9 a.m. to 12 midnight through Sept. 18.

Analysis

1. The title promises intriguing reading.

2. Paragraph one tells of Disneyland's fabulous drawing power.

3. Most readers will find the statistics amazing—the park contains a 235-room hotel, 20 restaurants and "refreshment corners," and 160 acres—a quarter of a section —of land!

4. Disneyland contains a replica of the famous Swiss Matterhorn, complete with "snow," glacial grottoes, live mountain climbers, and even bobsled runs!

5. At Disneyland you can take a submarine cruise.

6. Two streamlined monorail trains carry an average of 100,000 passengers a week at Disneyland.

7. Disneyland has four multi-level Super-Autopias where thousands of people drive gasoline powered miniature sport cars for amusement.

8. The Circarama, utilizing 11 separate projectors and as many screens, gives a fast-moving tour of some of the more fascinating aspects of the United States.

Conclusion

It is clear that there is a family of travel articles. One type may show how to save time, another how to handle small children on a trip, another will depict a safe method of handling an automobile, and still another may sketch a fascinating place to visit. We have given examples of only a few of the many types of travel articles.

Travel is at an all-time high. And as the world becomes even more internationally-minded, travel is certain to increase. This, in my opinion, means that the demand for travel articles will grow and grow and grow. It well may be that the travel article has the very brightest future of them all. Learn to write it well. That can be of tremendous importance to you.

Chapter XII

THE PERSONAL EXPERIENCE ARTICLE

BEGINNING WRITERS seem to feel that in some far-flung spot they can find the most fascinating material for articles, and they probably can. But what about the material at hand? The facts, incidents, and personal experiences in your own life well may become the bases for many publishable—even significant—*personal experience articles*.

Be sure that you use this material. It may be for you, as it has been for other writers, acres of diamonds.

The personal experience article is one which reports an experience of the author. The range of subjects is infinite, the incidents reported may be 100% fact or they may be generously garnished with fiction. The articles themselves may be humorous, dramatic, or significant. The basic characteristic of this kind of article is that it reports a personal experience, and the more intimate that experience, other elements being equal, the better.

TYPES

Since the personal experience article you offer to a magazine must be the kind that periodical uses, it is essential that you recognize the various types. Here are some of them which seem to be in continual demand:

1. *Fillers.* This is a very short—300 words or less—article of slight importance but one containing entertainment value. For instance:

My wife and I expected amusing incidents when we took our city-bred daughters, Gaila, 5, and Jo Anne, 4, for their first vacation in the country. The girls were amazed at many things but the farm animals especially intrigued them.

"Oh," exclaimed Gaila as we drove away from a pony farm, "I wish I had a little horsey."

Jo Anne was unimpressed. "If you had one," she declared, "you couldn't operate it."

"I could so!" Gaila flared, eyes flashing.

Jo Anne remained unconvinced. "I'll bet," she scorned, "you couldn't even reverse it from the parking post!"

2. *Famous person article.* This article may recount an incident or a series of incidents in the life of a celebrity. Its purpose is not to sketch the famous person's career nor to glorify him but to inspire readers, to give them courage, to help them in their own major battles with life.

3. *Recovery article.* Such an article tells how an individual who has undergone some ailment—physical or mental—has fought his way back to a life of real usefulness and happiness. Sometimes these articles carry a by-line, but often they are anonymous. This means that you, the author, may ghost-write such articles.

4. *Family article.* Generally this consists of a parent telling a dramatic personal experience which he or she has undergone in relation to another member of the family. One such article narrates the story resulting from a three-year-old child's disappearance from her mountain

home. This made a full-length feature of interesting reading.

5. *Unique activity article.* In this kind of piece the writer reports an unusual activity of a man, woman, boy, or girl. The uniqueness of the activity seems to be a major factor in such an article. One such article tells of a hospital for birds.

6. *Philosophical article.* Often such articles deal with children and are written years after the recorded incident happened. For instance: "When Santa Claus Did Not Come," an article of this type, tells the author's keen disappointment on a long-ago Christmas morning. But it also reports how this incident contributed to the author's growing up, becoming a mature, well-balanced woman.

7. *Personal opinion article.* This type of article may report the author's total disagreement with something which is a generally accepted belief or practice. One such article points out that it is foolish for an individual to become a do-it-yourself-er. The author declares it is far cheaper and more satisfactory to let the mechanic repair your car, the plumber fix your sink, and the painter paint your house.

8. *Adventure story.* A perennial favorite among the men's magazines, this type of story also appears in juvenile publications, general family periodicals, and even in women's magazines. The article may deal with any subject under the sun so long as it is truly dramatic, and, if the story is not dramatic, you may as well not write it.

9. *Personality article.* This tells of one who had an unfortunate personality, has suffered as a result, awakened to the horrible truth, taken corrective measures, and is

now quite happy. There are hundreds of variations of this theme. It is a favorite among women's magazines, and it also appears in the so-called personality books. It seldom appears in a men's publication.

10. *Strange psychic experience article.* This often takes the form of a ghost story. It appears from time to time in various magazines. Some publications frequently use this type of story which often concerns extrasensory perception, the field in which Dr. J. B. Rhine of Duke University has worked so successfully.

INGREDIENTS

Regardless of the type of personal experience article you write, it must contain certain ingredients if it is to sell. Among the necessary elements are:

1. The appearance of truth. Seldom will an editor buy an article unless it sounds true. That is, regardless of the truth of the story, it must be convincing. It must *sound* true.

2. Interest. Your article must be of such quality as to demand reader interest. See that what you have to say is of sufficient importance to snare and hold the reader's interest right down to the final period.

3. Intensely personal feeling. If you are an inhibited person who cannot tell in detail your feelings, aspirations, fears, loves, and hates, you will do well to avoid this type of article.

4. Humanitarianism. If you can inject this element into a personal experience article, you will help yourself to a sale. This is one of the really big sales factors in the personal experience article.

5. Vivid writing. Never be satisfied with the cliché. Strive to produce fresh, original writing. Make your article as bright and forceful as possible.

6. Public figure. The more newsworthy the person you write about, the more likely—other elements being equal —you are to sell your article.

7. Emotion. Emotion is absolutely necessary in the personal experience article, and the stronger the emotion, the better.

8. Suspense. Articles of this kind should be suspenseful. This means that you should deliberately plan them so they will contain a generous portion of suspense. Keep your reader's mind racing ahead to see what happens next. This is a potent sales device.

MARKETS

There is hardly a magazine published which will refuse a personal experience article tailored to its needs. And there is not a periodical that will buy an article which does not fit its needs. Your problem, therefore, is to understand exactly what a given publication uses. Perhaps the best way to approach this problem is to analyze one type of personal experience article to show you how to determine the kind of personal experience article a particular magazine will buy.

The Family Article

You may be surprised to learn that religious publications use many personal experience articles. Not long ago *Home Life* published the following personal experience article:

MY DAD WAS AN IMPOSSIBLE CASE *

By His Daughter

It was Promotion Day, the last Sunday in September. The church I was attending was in the midst of a revival. The evangelist was conducting a special service in the Intermediate department where I was a visitor.

I was sixteen and had just graduated from high school. I did not know then that these were unusual services. It was my first Sunday at Sunday school since I was a little child, when the neighbors took me occasionally. I had also responded that Sunday to the invitation of a neighbor, a crippled lady who lived near us.

Little did I realize when I accepted that invitation what was in store for me that day. My whole life was completely changed by the things I learned in two brief hours! It was the first time I had ever heard the plan of salvation. It struck me like a bolt of lightning. I responded to it with my whole being.

We were a large family—mother, father, and several children. Not one in the family was a Christian. Dad was generally regarded as an atheist. For some reason—I do not know why—he was very bitter against churches, against preachers, against Christians. He did not believe in the deity of Christ. He was his own god.

How well I remember his quoting William Henley's *Invictus:* "I am the master of my fate: I am the captain of my soul"—always with the emphasis on "I." Then he would straighten his shoulders, throw back his head, and say that his head, too, was "bloody, but unbowed."

He drank heavily at times, and cursing was his natural language. To this day, I cannot hear the name "Jesus Christ" without wincing. When he drank, he was always very quiet.

The family was seated around the table when I came home from church that day. As soon as I took my seat at the table, I told them that I had become a Christian. I shall never forget my dad's response! "Go upstairs and read Ingersoll's *Sixty-one Reasons for Doubting the Inspiration of the Bible.*" He made me feel as if I had committed a terrible sin.

I left the table sobbing, and I remember that I had a splitting headache all afternoon. I resolved then that I would try to convince my dad that there was something to what I had experienced. I had experienced it, and he hadn't! How could he know what I was talking about when he hadn't experienced it, and how could he tell me that I didn't know? My experience was real to me, and I felt that he had no right to try to make me deny it.

Three months later I united with the church and was baptized. How I longed for my mother and dad to be with me that night, but neither was present. My two younger sisters attended regularly with me, and it wasn't long until they followed in my footsteps.

We were very happy in our church relationship. It was something we had needed, but hadn't known where to find it. How indebted I am to that Sunday school teacher and that pastor who stayed with me through those trying months!

Every Sunday I heard a debate—the affirmative presented by the Sunday school teacher and pastor, the negative presented by my dad. It is strange, however, that during this time Dad quit his drinking, and he never cursed again in my presence.

I took Dad as my "project." To win him became my purpose in life. I felt that the other members of the family would follow if he would lead, for he had a tremendous influence on all of us.

I enlisted the help of my young friends at the church. Our young people were organized into a soul-winning group, and we often went into the homes of the unsaved and the shut-ins and held services. We always had group singing, prayer, Scripture reading, and a devotion.

Several times we had services in our home, and my dad and mother always listened attentively and expressed their appreciation. I remember how I always led in prayer, even though I trembled as I did for fear my father would think I was "beside myself." I had heard him talk about others who prayed, and I knew that his feeling for them was not one of admiration.

I shared my concern for my parents with every pastor our church had. Every one of them, I believe, was burdened for my mother and dad, and each one tried to win them. Always during revivals I talked with the visiting preachers. Many of them visited in our home and talked at length with my parents.

I have talked with hundreds of praying people and enlisted their co-operation. Perhaps they grew tired of hearing my oft-repeated request for prayer for my family—but at the time I was not concerned about that.

I have been privileged to work in various Baptist offices, including two churches. I have had close association with many outstanding preachers and leaders. Their wonderful faith has encouraged me and strengthened my own faith, and enabled me to cope with Dad's questions and doubts.

Dad has been the most difficult case I have ever known. I am not the only one who feels that way. Many have told me that he would never be won. How sad it is that so many have had to pay such a price for his stubborn rebellion against God.

Finally, when Dad was seventy-eight years of age, both my younger sister, who was a Christian, and my mother, who was not, became seriously ill. During this time, my mother made her profession quietly in the home with the help of a dear friend. Not long after that, God called home my sister.

This broke Dad's heart, and he finally bowed his head. He wept constantly, and he could not face people. I knew what was wrong, and I asked him to attend church with me. He finally agreed.

During the entire service he was moving, twisting, and turning, crossing and uncrossing his legs. When the invitation was given, I whispered, "Dad, would you like to go?"

He answered, "Not tonight."

The following Sunday night he attended again, and the very instant the invitation hymn was started, he whispered to me, "Do you *want* me to go?"

Did I want him to go!

O God, if he only knew how all my Christian life I had yearned for this moment. If he only knew of the agonizing prayer in his behalf. If he only knew the embarrassment he had caused his family. If he only knew of the sleepless nights I had spent. If he only knew of the times I had awakened from a dream, terrified, because I had seen his soul in hell. Did I want him to go!

Our entire congregation was electrified that night as this weeping, repentant, trembling father of mine stepped out from his place and hurried to the front to make his profession of faith. I shook with mixed emotions. Our life as a family came back to me. His life flashed across my mind, and my own life was relived, all in a moment.

The power of God has been demonstrated in a marvelous way in Dad's life, just as it is demonstrated every time a soul is saved. In his case, however, the change is so great it is almost unbelievable. Truly, he is "a new creature." Selfishness has been transformed into unselfishness; rebellion has become humility; neglect has been changed to concern and helpfulness.

Today, twenty-six years after becoming a Christian, I feel as if I have been running a long, long race and have finally reached the finish line. The Scriptures have become very real to me. My faith has been greatly strengthened, although I must admit there were times when it wavered and almost flickered out.

And I believe that the same power that transformed Dad will one day change my two brothers—whose spirit of unbelief is quite the same as his once was.

Analysis

Why did this article appeal to *Home Life*? Let us examine it for the purpose of discovering its specific appeals. We find that it:

1. Is a girl's story about her father. Certainly she is in a position to give valid information on this subject. And she does give pertinent, intimate, and even unpraiseworthy information about her father. This helps to make the article sound true.

2. Has a reasonable opening. You are entirely ready to accept the daughter's statements as fact. She gives details and motivations which ring true.

3. Gets off to a fast start. By the end of paragraph 4 the reader understands the situation, knows it has the potentialities of a good story, and is ready to follow it to the end.

4. Intensifies as it advances. The father, an atheist, sends his daughter to read Bob Ingersoll's famous discourse attacking the inspiration of the Bible, and the daughter, deeply hurt, resolves to change her father's attitude about the deity.

5. Shows what the daughter did to change her father's outlook on religion. And, little by little—but not too rapidly—the reader sees the daughter winning.

6. Gets in a "plug" for the Baptists. (*Home Life* is a Baptist publication.)

7. Shows the mother of the author professing Christianity and doing so in a convincing manner.

8. Depicts the author doing her utmost to persuade her father to become a Christian. This continued over the years and included the prayers and aid of friends, former ministers, present ministers, and perhaps others.

9. Reports a thrilling climax. "Do you *want* me to go?" the father asked his daughter when the invitational hymn was played at church on a Sunday evening.

Did I want him to go!

This is a splendid example of emotion. And also, in other parts of the article are many other similar uses of this powerful literary tool.

10. Expresses the author's superlative happiness resulting from her father's action.

Comment

Here is a skillfully written article. It is aimed at a particular audience—families of individuals who regularly attend church. Notwithstanding this fact, the author took time and effort to supply details which make the article sound entirely true. Beyond all doubt most readers found the article absolutely convincing.

Another fact which gives this article force is the direct discourse it contains. It is far more forceful to quote a character than to translate his words into your own statement. And, if you will note, the author used direct discourse at the high points of interest in the article. This is as it should be.

On occasion the author, utilizing a device of fiction

writers, went into the mind of the heroine—herself, in this case. Here we read: *"O, God, if he only knew how all my Christian life I had yearned for this moment. If he only knew of the agonizing prayers in his behalf. If he only knew the embarrassment he had caused his family . . ."*

You will note that this article appears in chronological order. But you must also realize that the author, in selecting the incidents to report, chose those which will contribute to the effect she desired to produce. As a result, the interest in the story increases as the tale progresses.

And finally, the end of the article is entirely satisfactory. It—as editors say—"comes off." The author knew the sweet fruit of victory—a victory which made her readers quite happy, indeed.

Here, then, is a really excellent model for you to study. Learn well the techniques which this author utilized so adeptly. They can help you to sell innumerable articles of your own creation.

No matter who you are, what your educational, economic, or social position, you doubtless have in your own life material for dozens of genuinely helpful personal experience articles. Your business is to recognize this material and put it into salable form.

Chapter XIII

THE PROFILE

••

PERHAPS YOU are one of those writers who, although glad to sell material to the smaller magazines, propose to use them as a bridge to the more pretentious publications. Thousands of your predecessors have done this, even more are doing it, and you may do it, too.

Here is one way: Write for the small magazines a type of feature which is in constant demand by the big popular magazines. Write these so convincingly, so vividly, so forcefully that they will demand the attention of mass circulation periodicals.

What type article? I suggest the profile as an especially propitious choice.

A profile is more than a one-sided sketch of a personality. It reveals far more than highlights and shadows. A well-done profile shows the inner workings of the subject's mind, his loves and his hates, kindnesses and cruelties, bigness and smallness. A profile is a full-length portrait and, at its best, it can portray a profession, a city, or even an era.

The demand for the really well-done profile is tremendous. This is understandable because its subject generally is the ever-fascinating, often all but incomprehensible human being. In the profile you will see what makes one become a nonentity or a Somerset Maugham, a Rita Hayworth, or a Jacqueline Kennedy. It is small wonder that the profile has been called the world's most fascinating article.

How-To-Do-It

How does one write the profile?

First, you must know the ingredients of a profile. Among them are:

1. Proper slant

Slant your article for the magazine which you hope will buy the story.

2. Wealth of anecdotes

See that the anecdotes you include in your article reveal character. They should show the kind of individual you are writing about. And the greater insight they give into the character himself the better. Finally, the anecdotes must be an integral part of the article.

3. Quotations from the subject

According to an editor of a leading men's magazine, the most important aspect of the profile is making the subject come alive for the reader.

"This comes about," he says, "largely through an accumulation of seemingly unimportant details, an accurate reproduction of the man's way of speaking, and a series of anecdotes which reveal his character."

4. Subject's peculiarities

Record the subject's personality quirks and oddities. These will consist of intriguing unknown facts—of all kinds—about the subject. You should include absurdities as well as profundities in the subject's make-up.

5. Glimpse of the "inner man"

Your profile must contain an indication of what makes the subject the kind of person he is. For instance: In *Time* magazine there appeared a profile of Leonard Bernstein. It showed him as a man with a superabundance of energy and tremendous vitality. This article made it clear that he is a man of action. Much of Bernstein's versatility can be explained by this one psychological factor, this glimpse of the "inner man."

6. Complete honesty

Since no man is perfect, there must be in any profile indications of imperfection. You, the writer, must give both sides of the man's character. You must probe into the areas of his life which he would rather leave unmolested, find potent motivations, discover and report dramatic actions. These will do much toward making your article come alive.

7. Drama

Again you may help yourself to a sale if you put into the profile a number of realistic situations teeming with drama. These must be a part of your story, not something dragged in merely for the sake of drama.

8. Originality

You need not follow the rules—not even those outlined here—provided you tell the story forcefully, clearly, and effectively. Tell it in your own way but be sure that your reader, once he has begun to read the article, will not be satisfied to put down the magazine until he has finished your story. Fresh expressions, simple, direct language, and individuality will be helpful to you in producing originality in the profiles you write.

9. Constructiveness

If you can make your article constructive, you will thereby increase your chances to make a sale.

10. Climax

Your profile must reach a definite climax, and you must build to it just as if you were writing a fiction story. The article and the fiction story are far more alike than many writers seem to think. Each should move swiftly toward a crashing climax.

MARKETS

No matter how expert you may be as a writer, you must slant your profile for a particular market if you hope to sell it. For instance, *Together,* the Methodist publication, would hardly be interested in a profile dealing with John Dillinger, no matter how well written. Neither would *Playboy* be likely to buy a story dealing with Carry Nation.

You must study your markets and produce material that will fit into the schedule of a given publication. To that end, let us look at a few specific publications.

Religious Magazines

Your market tips will tell you that *Together* is interested in articles up to 2,000 words in length on personal experiences in home problems and community affairs, in church and religious life. This includes the profile, of which the following is a good example:

MANY LOOK, FEW SEE *

By Herman B. Teeter

In Mexico a few years ago an entire town exploded in excitement when an elderly woman, loaded with cameras, climbed out on a belfry and slid along the high ridge of a church roof.

"I was merely trying," she explained later, "to get a better angle on that beautiful cathedral at the other end of the street."

This was the same woman who has chased kangaroos in Australia, surf riders in Hawaii, insects and flowers in Illinois. She's Mrs. Myrtle R. Walgreen, 79, and a widow. In the years since she was 60, she has photographed everything from the top of a rainbow (out of a plane) to the heart of a Christmas rose in December snow.

By plane, auto, ship, and afoot, Mrs. Walgreen has traveled the world over many times—but always she returns to her Hazelwood estate, a lovely spot of earth near Chicago where 250 acres of unspoiled woodland spill down a cliff to the brink of Rock River.

Close friends insist she should have been a boy. This is suggested, no doubt, by a sense of small-boy wonder which prompts her to collect unusual objects from all over the world.

When the Walgreen maids open a refrigerator they aren't surprised at whatever they find, even—as has happened—a tree frog slumbering in artificially induced hibernation. And one of her photographic subjects—a four-foot snake—once escaped to roam the house for a day and a night. Yet Myrtle Walgreen is the most feminine of women.

In her person are combined a zest for living—and looking —with widely recognized talents as a photographer. She has

won some 500 awards for her color pictures—of which she
has 12,000, carefully sorted and indexed. She is in demand as
a slide-show lecturer, but her fees, ranging up to $100, never
cross her palm. They go directly to Chicago's Red Cross, of
which she is an executive.

For this great-grandmother, the world is full of adventure—
an adventure that took on new dimensions comparatively late
in life. As a result, she is sometimes referred to as the "da
Vinci of the color camera" or "that amazing dowager."

Her pictures are striking because they take a look at the
world as few people see it. When she looks for beauty, she
finds it everywhere—in an ant's eye view of mushrooms that
glow at night, or in milkweed seeds ready for flight. After one
of Mrs. Walgreen's recent illustrated lectures, a Chicago club
woman remarked:

"I have the feeling I've been blind most of my life. It was as
if I had put on glasses for the first time. Things gained a
sudden new depth and clarity."

A hearty person with a ready laugh, Mrs. Walgreen pursues
her subjects with the diligence and initiative of a crack news
photographer. As she nears 80, her enthusiasm, stamina, and
love of life are as great as those of many middle-agers.

A few winters ago, in five-below-zero weather, police de-
toured her automobile around a burning building in Chicago.
She stopped, then walked several blocks to catch the frigid
beauty of ice-coated fire-fighters and their equipment.

"It was so cold," she recalls, "that my camera froze up
repeatedly. Each time I'd have to go back to the car to thaw
it out."

The picture she made, "Frozen In", has hung in salons with
her shots of snail shells, poppy seeds, ripe buckeyes, okra pods,
potato sprouts, desert sunsets, and water lilies.

Born in Carbondale, Illinois, she was married to Charles
Walgreen, an enterprising young druggest, in 1902. Together

they saw their drugstore chain grow until today it numbers nearly 500 Walgreen stores and some 2,000 agency stores. Walgreen's system of expansion was a simple one, she points out:

"Every now and then my husband would come home and say, 'Myrtle, I've found a man smarter than I am. I'm going to set him up in a drugstore.' "

And when her husband began pioneering the drugstore lunch counter, it was his wife who first took over in her own kitchen, making chicken salad, soups, and pies.

A Methodist, as she puts it, "from cradle-roll days," she's a trustee of the First Methodist Church of Chicago, a downtown skyscraper church known as the Chicago Temple. As a memorial to her husband, she gave the funds for building the Chapel in the Sky, which was dedicated in 1952. Steel girders near the top of the tall building were encased in oak, part of which was hewn from great trees at Hazelwood. A beautiful altar sculpture shows "Christ Looking at Chicago."

Her golden years are full, often from early morning to well into the night. She has wealth, but insists money is not essential to happiness. Her hobby of photography costs little more than she would spend for cigarettes—and she doesn't smoke.

"There is no reason," she feels, "for a woman left alone by the death of a husband and the marriage of children to lead a lonely life. Too many women lead dreary, waiting-for-the-end-existences simply because they have mistaken ideas. For me, these last years have been rich with stimulating experiences."

During the week, she lives in a Chicago apartment overlooking Lake Michigan. But each weekend finds her at Hazelwood, which is both a forest preserve and vast flower garden. Mrs. Walgreen didn't take up gardening until she was 50. Now this interest in flowers shows up in many of her prize-winning photographs.

Her philanthropies are many. For over 20 years she has

sponsored the Beautification of Home Grounds 4-H Club project, awarding four gold pins to winners in each county of the U.S. and gold watches to winners in each state. Each year, too, she pays the expenses of eight 4-H finalists on a week-long stay in Chicago. In addition, she is exceptionally active in her garden clubs. And as a Fellow of the Photographic Society of America, she's often called on to judge photographs at color salons.

One contestant observed her as she selected projected pictures, commenting expertly on each.

"I sure do like the way that old lady judges," he remarked.

It is typical of Myrtle Walgreen that she considers this comment one of the nicest compliments she has ever received.

Analysis

Why did this story appeal to *Together,* one of the better-paying magazines in this field? Perhaps the following facts had a material bearing on the editor's decision to purchase this article:

1. The author makes his subject intriguing. He shows her—Mrs. Myrtle R. Walgreen—climbing out of a belfry, sliding along a ridge pole high above the ground, in order to get a shot of a beautiful cathedral. He tells us that she is a world traveler who is likely to bring home insects, frogs, snakes.

2. Mrs. Walgreen is worthy of emulation. She is a photographer of considerable note, a competent lecturer, and something of a philanthropist. Although 79 years of age, she is still interested in life and finds the world full of adventure.

3. Her family connections are interesting. It was her husband, Charles Walgreen, an enterprising young druggist, who built the famous Walgreen chain of drug stores.

Mrs. Walgreen pioneered with her husband in the drug-store lunch counter business.

4. Mrs. Walgreen is a Methodist. This, for a Methodist publication, certainly helps to make the article acceptable.

5. The article is constructive. It points out that money is not the source of happiness, nor is it necessary for a woman, simply because she is a widow whose children are married, to lead a lonely life.

6. Mrs. Walgreen's entire activities are permeated with the principles of Christianity. "Her reverent labor of love at 79," the article reports in a photograph caption, "opens the eyes of others to the God-given wonders of the world around us."

7. The photographs, taken by Mrs. Walgreen and used as illustrations in this article, are truly spectacular. They emphasize the "countless daily miracles found along God's wonderful trailside world." This, for a religious magazine, certainly is a big selling point.

8. Despite the brevity of this article, you get a fairly complete idea of what Mrs. Walgreen is like. You feel as if you are beginning to know her.

9. This article has family appeal. It will interest the children, young adults, and persons who are approaching their "golden years."

10. This article leaves with the reader a wholesome view of life, a feeling that God is in His heaven and all is well with the world.

Comment

Suppose you had been editor of *Together* when Herman Teeter offered "Many Look, Few See" for publication. Would you have bought it?

Before you answer that question, you may want to consider that this article:

1. Is interesting in itself.

2. Offers practical suggestions to individuals who are beyond the years of strenuous activity.

3. Contains no element to which any person could reasonably object.

4. Has spectacular and appropriate photographs for illustrations.

5. Tends to document the teachings of Christianity.

6. Ends in a satisfactory manner.

With these facts in mind, could you reject the manuscript? Hardly. Neither did the editor. In fact, he commented editorially about this article, blurbed it on the front cover, and even used one of Mrs. Walgreen's spectacular color shots on the cover!

When you produce comparable offerings, you will meet with identical treatment at the hands of editors. Your business is to give the editor so many things that appeal to his readers—and so few things to which his readers would object—that he will feel that the article is tailored to his publication.

How do you do that? The rules are simple. Understand the audience, know the men and women who read the magazine which you hope will buy your story. Know why they read that publication. Then, put into your article the very things these readers want.

Trade Journals

Do the trade journals use profiles? Indeed they do! According to one of the country's leading trade journalists,

"There will be nearly three times as many (trade journals) published during the Soaring Sixties as there were during the last decade."

This is a rosy picture for the trade journal writer who learns his business and practices it. And an excellent way to begin is via the profile.

Just what do these journals use in the way of profiles?

Boot and Shoe Recorder is interested in feature articles, including profiles, up to 2,000 words in length. Here is such an article from that publication:

PROFILE *

By Estelle G. Anderson

A small seashell and Number 26 on his calling card immediately identify the man and his interests. Abraham (Ab) Rosenberg is a conchologist. He used to spend his spare time walking the sandy beaches of Key West and Coral Gables in Florida, where he lives, looking for the "gifts of the sea." But he hasn't had much opportunity to pick seashells during the past six months, because of Number 26. He is completely engrossed, enthused and dedicated to No. 26; and if by any chance you don't know what No. 26 is, he will tell you. "It is the functional shoe for children being made by the Precision Shoe Company, a Division of Genesco in Nashville, Tennessee."

Ab Rosenberg has been concerned with children's feet and fitting for the past 32 years. His contribution . . . originating new methods for fitting children's feet so as to give a base for healthy development. "That's why I am so excited about No. 26," he says.

"Here I am, in the last stretch of my business career, returning to children's shoes, with additional background in

* Reprinted by permission of *Boot and Shoe Recorder*.

many fields, especially merchandising and retailing. At this point, No. 26 represents the finest contribution I have seen made in the children's shoe field. It represents fulfillment of an opportunity to further children's foot health. If I had it to do all over again, I would do my part of it exactly the same way."

To get to the present, we must start with the past, and the time in 1924, when Ab Rosenberg graduated from New York University and went into the advertising department at Macy's in New York. Four years later, he switched to merchandising and went through each progressive step: Head of stock, assistant buyer and, in 1931, buyer of children's shoes. What a time to become head of a department, at the start of the greatest depression we have ever had. However, while over-all store sales volume declined from $100 million to $74 million, the children's shoe operation went from one-half to nearly one million dollars. Why? Ab explained: "Because we dedicated ourselves to children's foot health. That is when we introduced many innovations and the personalized fitting services that have continued through the years.

"We introduced the Fitting Counsellors, men of superior aptitude and qualifications. We trained them in our own school of fitting (a program that preceded similar ones across the country now, by some 28 years). Wherever you look today, across the land, you will find Macy graduates heading some of the biggest stores and excelling in businesses of their own.

"At Macy's, we developed our own shoe—the Gro-Shoe— the most widely known brand of children's shoes in the metropolitan area at that time. This was a quality shoe, made to our specifications, over lasts which we approved. We followed it up with a four-way method of fitting.

"We also instituted the Fitting Register. Here's how it worked. At the end of each sale we recorded the case history of each child: Name, address, date of birth, date of purchase, what

kind of shoes were fitted, the posture, the gait, the clerk and
supervisor's names. When the customer came in, we would
ask: 'Is your child registered with us?'

"The clerk would get the card and we were able to proceed
with a case history of pertinent information in hand. Ad-
ditionally, these cards served as reminders. Every three months,
we would write to the customer and suggest that perhaps she
should bring her child in for a recheck.

"This is a common practice now, but at that time it was
resisted. This was Macy's . . . not a specialty store with some
200 customers but a gigantic operation, a massive organization.
But rewards came when customers said: 'This is what brought
me all the way to Macy's.' Parents came from far and wide to
the crossroads . . . Macy's . . . because they knew their children would be fitted properly and they could believe this would
help their children to have healthy feet."

Years later, when Macy's bought Bamberger's, Ab took over
both the Macy's and Bamberger children's shoe operations.
He dramatized the Gro-Shoe, put visual displays on the walls
and out in the center of the floor. Thus the Fitting Register
grew to about 85,000 children.

Shortly afterwards, George Farkas, a boyhood friend, invited Ab to join him at Alexander's. They had two small
stores, one at 152nd Street and the other at the Grand Con-
course in the Bronx. They were family controlled and directed;
but their concept was great . . . a fashion discount operation.

Ab Rosenberg recognized the great potential of discount
stores back in '38. At Alexander's he directed merchandising,
personnel development and participated in top-level planning.
His purpose was to change the stores to a corporate operation;
to gear them for big business . . . in the way department stores
were operating at the time.

However, he could never stay out of the children's shoe
department. Here was a need and an attraction, so he paid

more than ordinary attention to the development of that department.

It was a question of starting from the ground up. No Macy source would sell Alexander's. It meant building a store brand again . . . Foot Guider. This marked the beginning of another children's shoe achievement; and the growth has continued with the phenomenal rise of the store.

At Alexander's, Ab created the fitting platform. The display director of the store, Irving Blum, became the designer for Ab's idea of the Posture Study and Fitting Platform on which they did the following:

(1). Foot examination

(2). Gait analysis

(3). Size re-check

(4). X-ray inspection. This was a new method for studying feet and fit at an efficient level, where the fitting supervisor, without stooping, bending or peering between chairs and stools, could determine whether the shoe fitted and was suited to the gait and posture of the child . . . and the shoe could be viewed openly by the parent as well.

"Good fit is the most important ingredient in a children's shoe business," says Ab. "It requires a dedication to the welfare of each child, an understanding of what is correct for the posture, gait and shape of the moving foot. The aim . . . to help each young one to grow up with healthy feet. That's the only way."

In 1946, Ab became the head of another Farkas venture, Hartley's, then the largest specialty store operation in the State of Florida. Here, he was Board Chairman and partner. It became a living symbol of the slogan he created: "The Heart of Fashion in Tropical America."

All of Ab's tools of the trade . . . the Fitting Register, Fitting Supervisor, the Fitting Platform . . . were introduced to Florida, through Hartley's. Bernard Kanter, one of Ab's alumni of the Macy School of Fitting Supervisors, joined him. "He was a brilliant star," says Ab. "They were all dedicated fitters, and wonderful people. They are buyers, merchandise men, store heads and store owners today."

Hartley's was sold in 1951, and after six months of leisure, Ab felt he wanted to get back into business. He joined up with Fred Lazarus, Jr. Became vice-president in charge of soft lines merchandising in Federated Department Stores' new venture, Fedway Stores. All they had was money, $23,000,000; and they set about opening eight stores from Texas to California.

Once again, children's shoes received special emphasis. Every blueprint was another opportunity for building a children's shoe business. All of the proven devices were used again. In connection with the fitting platform, they added murals to dramatize and depict Steps 1 to 4.

They also introduced the Mez-u-rite fitting instrument. It worked like a bathroom scale. You stood on it, with both feet, moved the lever; and it registered the size. The fitting platform had taught that the effective level for checking feet was 30 inches above the ground.

They went one step further now. Children, one and two years old, were not easily served in regular chairs. So another platform level was created on which they put little chairs. This was specialized furniture, for the children's department. "Through Fedway Stores we were once more spreading the gospel," says Ab. "We were preaching the new tools for fitting children's feet, from Texas to California."

When Fedway Stores was reorganized in 1954, Ab Rosenberg went into the field of consulting, not specifically on children's shoes, until May 1959, when he did a survey for the International Shoe Company in their Florida operations, at Jordan Marsh and Maas Brothers. Here, again, the professional tools, Fitting Platform, Fitting Register, Mez-u-rite Fitting, specialized chairs for babies, murals, were put into practice. In addition, there was the visual display technique: Setting out the assortment of shoe styles, so that the customer can see at a glance what is available. A self-selection technique, similar to the supermarket, so the customer can pre-select her choice.

Which brings us up to November 1959, when Ab Rosenberg became interested in functional shoes and Number 26. Now you know why he said if he had it to do all over again, he would not change a single thing.

This "profile" may be somewhat lengthy; but after all, it does represent some thirty-five years, every one of them dedicated to children's foot health.

Ab Rosenberg could have gone on and on about the personal aspects of this biographical sketch. He is so very proud of his wife, Lois. She is a professional artist. Has shown her paintings at New York art galleries. "She is wonderful with people," says Ab, "a remarkable wife, mother and grandmother."

They have one grandson. Ab beamed when he talked about his three sons, Albert, Arthur, Allen, each one an individual entity and personality. All of them talented, dynamic and capable in their chosen professions.

Analysis

Before we begin to weigh the value of that article, let us look at *Boot and Shoe Recorder*. An 80-page magazine, well printed on coated paper, it advertises all kinds of footwear, trade shows, and shoe machinery.

The table of contents of a typical issue includes the following titles: "Voice of the Trade," "Profile—Abraham L. Rosenberg," "Pattern Portrait: Lightweight Patio Style," "College Styles Come Two Ways," and "Shoes and the Consumer."

This clearly establishes the purpose of the magazine—*to help the shoe retailer*. With this in mind, we may examine the profile in an effort to see why the editor bought the article. We note that it:

1. Concerns a prominent figure in the shoe industry— a man who is an authority on the subject of merchandising children's shoes.

2. Gives information about a new functional shoe which is of considerable interest to the industry, particularly to retailers.

3. Reports Rosenberg's career in the shoe business, showing that even under adverse conditions, he was able to sell shoes. Since the article reports successful methods which others may use, we must classify it as constructive.

4. Gives a bit of advice from this national authority: "We dedicated ourselves to children's foot health," he says. "That is when we introduced many innovations and the personalized fitting service that has continued through the years."

5. Tells the story of the Fitting Counsellors, a merchandising device which Rosenberg used with marked success.

6. Cites a successful shoe merchandising method—the Fitting Register—and reports how it worked.

7. Outlines the story of the Fitting Platform and gives details about it as a means to better shoe retailing.

8. Sketches the story of Mez-u-rite, a fitting instrument, used as a means of better customer service.

9. Tends to advertise a *Boot and Shoe Recorder* advertiser—the same issue which carries this profile contains a full page of advertising about No. 26.

10. Is packed with information which will be of real

value to the retail shoe merchant, especially the man engaged in the children's shoe business.

Comment

It is hardly surprising that *Boot and Shoe Recorder* published the Rosenberg profile. Every one of the points listed in the foregoing analysis is a sound reason why it appealed to the editor whose business is to help a particular segment of people—those engaged in the shoe business. Since this profile contributed to that end, writer Anderson sold her article.

Conclusion

Here, then, we have a Methodist magazine containing the profile story of a noted Methodist; and *Boot and Shoe Recorder* outlining the history of a leader in the shoe merchandising business. These profiles are blueprints to sales. They may lead you step by step through the portals of the biggest and highest-paying magazines published, into a fascinating world, into the very minds and souls of the most noted men and women in the world today.

Chapter XIV

THE SIGNIFICANT ARTICLE

•••

WHEN you have attained a certain proficiency in article building, you may feel a dissatisfaction in your achievement. Like Alexander the Great, you may have a desire to conquer other worlds. If you accept this challenge, tackle the problem intelligently, and work at it seriously, you can succeed. And that success can far transcend any other you have known.

In order to reach this peak of achievement, you must give direction to your efforts. You cannot become a Don Quixote and furiously ride off in all directions. Rather, of all possible courses of action, you must choose one and pursue it with steadfast purpose.

What shall that be? In which direction shall you ride?

This depends upon you. But I wish to offer a suggestion.

You are a professional writer and, as such, keenly aware of the vast differences in articles. Some of them, you note, in addition to being well organized and skillfully written contain a quality which lifts them into a realm far beyond the run-of-the-mine article.

These distinguished articles have a timelessness, an element which lodges in your brain and refuses to depart, a something which is particularly applicable to your own life. For want of a more accurate term, we shall call this element *significance*.

Realizing these facts, you may desire to produce not merely articles which will sell, but minor masterpieces of significance. This is one direction you may go in your professional writing. And whether it brings you fame and fortune—or neither—it can become the most rewarding experience of your life.

INGREDIENTS

Precisely what gives an article significance?

Perhaps we can best answer this question by setting down some of the ingredients which contribute to that end. Among them are the following:

1. A big subject. It is difficult to imagine a significant article about an unimportant subject—a postage stamp, no matter how rare, for example. But the effect of Christian principles on world leaders very well might become the basis for a highly significant article.

2. Honesty. Propaganda has no place in this type of article. It can contain no half-truths, no partially explored facets, no minimizing of the unpleasant or exaggerating of the pleasant to achieve an effect. The article must be candid, factual, and entirely valid throughout.

3. Universality. A significant article can hardly be one which will affect only a small number of people. Instead, it should provide a vast number of individuals with a means for major improvements in their associations, businesses, and way of life.

4. Sound logic. The facts reported in the article must, without question, completely support the conclusion drawn.

5. Timeliness.

6. Simplicity. There are those who seem to feel that

they must deal with big subjects in a complex manner. This is erroneous reasoning. I cannot point to a single article of this nature that is actually significant. Undoubtedly simplicity contributes to significance.

7. Action inciting. No matter how skillfully you may write an article, unless it causes the reader to act on your suggestion, the article cannot be significant.

8. Basic in its concepts. When you set about producing a profoundly moving article, you must deal with fundamentals. In other words, go to rock bottom and begin there. Build your article on unshakable foundations.

9. Restraint. In some articles it is well enough to build up an emotion through various tricks which you have at your command. Not so in the significant article. Present your facts with restraint. That is far more effective than even the slightest straining to achieve an effect.

10. Constructiveness. It is not enough to point to the grave danger which a group of individuals face. This is only crying out with alarm and, however valuable that may be, it becomes significant only when you offer a solution, a means of avoiding the dire catastrophe which appears to lurk before them.

If you incorporate the foregoing ingredients, or a considerable number of them, into your article, you will be helping yourself toward the writer's greatest objective— the production of an article that is truly significant. It is this element which makes an article valuable both to the writer and the reader.

Such articles should offer material which is new to the majority of the readers of the particular magazine for which it is aimed. Is there a secret to the writing of articles of significance? Not a secret but a fact which few new writers understand: Editors weigh articles not in pounds and ounces, but on a scale of their value to the reader. A skilled editor can quickly tell the value of a given article to his readers, and if the value is low, the author gets a rejection slip. But if the audience-value of the article is high, the author gets a check.

Therefore, it is wise to do some careful editorial weighing in planning and writing your articles. You should try to develop your editorial powers to the limit so that you will include elements of significance in each article you write. In this way, you, the editor, and the audience will be delighted with the results.

MARKETS

Do the small magazines publish such articles? They do —in abundance. No magazine, simply because it is small, will reject a significant article. And it well may be that more significant articles appear in the small magazines than in the big popular publications. The latter, however, are also very much in the market for this type of article. Thus, by producing significant articles, you can enlarge your market and increase your rates of payment. And, what is far more important, really help your fellow man.

As an example of an article of significance published in a small magazine, let us turn to an article which was published in a business publication, *Forbes* magazine, and examine it carefully.

TRY GIVING YOURSELF AWAY *

By David Dunn

Like most people, I was brought up to look upon life as a process of getting. The idea of giving myself away came somewhat by accident. One night, lying awake in my berth on the Twentieth Century Limited en route to New York, I fell to wondering just where the Centuries passed each other that night.

"That would make a good subject for one of the New York Central's advertisements," I thought to myself—"Where the Centuries Pass." Next morning I wrote the New York Central Lines, outlining the idea and adding, "No strings attached." I received a courteous acknowledgment and the information that the Centuries passed near Athol Springs, N.Y., nine miles west of Buffalo.

Some months later I received a second letter informing me that my idea was to be the subject of the New York Central calendar for the new year. You may recall it: A night picture of the oncoming locomotive of one Century and the observation platform of the other, a scene rich in color and railroad romance.

That summer I traveled a good deal, and in almost every railroad station and hotel lobby and travel office I entered, even in Europe, hung *my* calendar. It never failed to give me a glow of pleasure.

It was then I made the important discovery that anything that makes one glow with pleasure is beyond money calculation in this world where there is altogether too much grubbing and too little glowing.

I began to experiment with giving-away and discovered it to be a lot of fun. If an idea of improving the window display of a neighborhood store flashes into my mind, I step in and

*Reprinted by permission of *Forbes* Magazine.

make the suggestion to the proprietor. If an incident occurs, the story of which I think the local Catholic priest could use, I call him up and tell him about it, though I am not a Catholic myself. If I run across an article some senator might want to read, I mail it to him. Sometimes I even send books to virtual strangers, when I feel sure they would be interested in a "find" I have made. Several fine friendships have been started in this way.

Successful giving-away has to be cultivated, just as does successful getting. Opportunities are as fleeting as opportunities for earning quick profits. But ideas in giving are like some varieties of flowers—the more you pick them, the more they bloom. And giving-away makes life so much more exciting that I strongly recommend it as a hobby. You need not worry if you lack money. Of all things a person may give away, money is the least permanent in the pleasure it produces and the most likely to backfire on the giver. Emerson was wise and practical when he wrote, "The only gift is a portion of thyself."

People have different things to give. Some have time, energy, skill, ideas. Others have some special talent. All of us can give away appreciation, interest, encouragement—which require no money expenditure unless for a postage stamp or a telephone call.

Of course you will be tempted to backslide. An idea popped into my head one day which I thought some department store might be able to use profitably. "Now *this* idea is worth money," I said to myself. "I'll try to sell it."

"You'll do nothing of the kind," said my wiser self. "You'll not spend your time peddling an idea; you'll give it away and get it out of your system."

So I wrote a letter to one of the world's most famous department stores, outlining the idea and presenting it to them. It was immediately adopted with appreciation, and now I have a big department store as a friend.

Simple appreciation is one of the most acceptable forms of giving-away. I have found that authors, actors, lecturers, public servants—even the biggest of them—are hungry for genuine expressions of approval. We think of them as being smothered with appreciation, whereas all too often they live on crumbs. The manufactured publicity that is created to promote them does not warm their hearts. What they crave is the spontaneous, human, friendly appreciation of the people they are trying to serve.

The other day I was in a hotel dining room where an orchestra was playing. It was a good orchestra, offering well-chosen selections, well-played. On the way out impulse prompted me to stop and say, "Gentlemen, I have thoroughly enjoyed your playing." For a second they looked almost startled. Then all of their faces broke into smiles, and I left them beaming over their instruments. My own day went off better for it, too.

Another discovery I have made is that it is almost impossible to give away anything in this world without getting something back—provided you are not *trying* to get something. Usually the return comes in some utterly unexpected form, and it is likely to be months or years later.

For example, one Sunday morning the local post office delivered an important special-delivery letter to my home, though it was addressed to me at my office, and the post office had discharged its obligation by attempting to deliver it there. I wrote the postmaster a note of appreciation. More than a year later I needed a post-office box for a new business I was starting. I was told at the window that there were no boxes left, that my name would have to go on a long waiting list. As I was about to leave, the postmaster appeared in the doorway. He had overheard the conversation. "Wasn't it you who wrote us that letter a year or so ago about delivering a special-delivery to your home?"

I said it was.

"Well, you certainly are going to have a box in this post office if we have to make one for you. You don't know what a letter like that means to us. We usually get nothing but kicks."

I had a box within the hour. Bread upon the waters!

After years of experience, this is how I have come to feel about my hobby: I have a job which pays me a living, so why should I try to drive a sharp bargain with the world for the extra ideas and impulses that come to me? I say let the world have them if they are of any value. I get my compensation out of feeling that I am a part of the life of my times, doing what I can to make things more interesting and exciting for other people. And that makes life more interesting and exciting for me, and keeps my mind keener.

As if this were not enough, I find that friends multiply and good things come to me from every direction. I've decided the world insists on balancing accounts with givers-away—provided their hands aren't outstretched for return favors.

Analysis

What is the basis of significance in a magazine article?

It appears to me that the element which makes an article significant is its helpfulness.

In our analysis, therefore, we shall attempt to discover those ingredients which helped to make this article helpful to you and me. We find it contains:

1. Original thinking. Who ever heard of giving away oneself? Yet this is exactly what the author recommends in this title. Also, the article makes it clear that if we practice this recommendation, we are certain to profit in one way or another—if we don't hold out our hand for a return favor.

2. Startling thesis. In reality, the author tells us that not only we, the readers, but those with whom we come in

contact, will be better off if we cooperate fully, freely, and without thought of return compensation.

3. Uncommon sense. To most of us the idea of giving something away—something of value—is abhorrent. We work for what we get and we should profit in a material way from our idea. But this article points out that the giver —provided he gives with no thought of a return favor— gets a priceless inner satisfaction from this action.

4. Help toward fuller living. "The only gift," Emerson wrote, "is a portion of thyself." The practice of this type of giving will result in a fuller, richer life to all who honestly indulge in it.

5. Everyday examples. Here we see no high-flown ideas which might be used by some unusual person on rare occasions. Rather, the author gives examples which anyone— regardless of his wealth or lack thereof—may use.

6. Tips to those who wish to try giving themselves away. "Successful giving-away," the author tells us, "has to be cultivated just as does successful getting. Opportunities are as fleeting as opportunities for earning quick profits."

7. Methods of procedure. You give yourself away spontaneously. It is something that you do quickly and it costs you little or nothing—a postage stamp, a telephone call, a smile, a word of appreciation.

8. Suggestions for having fun. Through this plan of giving yourself away, you may have fun. And, as there is altogether too little fun in most of our lives, this is an eminently worth-while objective.

9. Documentation of its ideas. The author experienced a "glow of pleasure" at seeing his calendar in hotel lobbies and train stations in many different countries. He found a

friend as a result of giving an idea to a department store. Because he was appreciative to the post office, he obtained a needed post-office box at once.

10. Stimulating ideas. We may—or may not—agree with author Dunn. But in either case, we can hardly read this article without giving serious thought to his argument. And that, in itself, is a helpful process. It stimulates our thinking. Too many of us need something to make us think and this article is certain to do that.

Comment

The history of this article is highly inspirational. It appeared first in *Forbes* magazine in June 1938—almost a quarter of a century ago! But it did not die. Something kept it alive in men's minds. And in August 1945—seven years later—*The Reader's Digest* reprinted it!

Two more years passed and the article was even more active. Author Dunn had expanded it into a book of the same title. And this book was so successful that, in 1956— almost two decades after the article appeared—the book was revised and republished!

Even that is not the end of this amazing story. At the special request of J. C. Penney, founder and director of the famous J. C. Penney Company chain of 1,700 stores, in August 1959, *The Reader's Digest* published this article for the *second* time.

"I know from long experience," Mr. Penney says, "that the philosophy of life set forth in this article actually works."

Because of these facts, I nominate *Try Giving Yourself Away* as a highly significant article. And more, I unequivocally declare that its significance is a direct result of the ingredients it contains.

How can you produce a significant article? Is there a guiding principle to follow? I think there is such a principle. It can mean the difference between complete failure and fantastic success. Here are its parts:

1. Subject matter in which *your audience* is very definitely interested.

2. Arresting title.

3. Fascinating opening sentence. If you are a careful writer, you will see that your initial sentence is of such a nature that your audience, upon reading it, will feel a strong mental urge to read on.

4. Article must march. It cannot be static and no part of it can be static.

5. Powerful message. There must be something in the article—an element really worth the reader's while—which will enable him to profit materially in some manner.

6. Potent climax. This will be the culmination of the article, the highest point of interest, and that should be something of monumental importance.

7. Satisfying conclusion. This will leave the reader with no unanswered questions. The article will be completely convincing.

The foregoing is a sketch of an ideal article. Few articles reach this ideal, but those few are invaluable to students of writing. Here, then, is such an article, a superb bit of craftsmanship which I recommend to you as an impressive model.

THE DAY AT THE BEACH *

By Arthur Gordon

Not long ago I came to one of those bleak periods that many of us encounter from time to time, a sudden drastic dip in the graph of living when everything goes stale and flat, energy wanes, enthusiasm dies. The effect on my work was frightening. Every morning I would clench my teeth and mutter: "Today life will take on some of its old meaning. You've got to break through this thing. You've got to!"

But the barren days went by, and the paralysis grew worse. The time came when I knew I had to have help.

The man I turned to was a doctor. Not a psychiatrist, just a doctor. He was older than I, and under his surface gruffness lay great wisdom and compassion. "I don't know what's wrong," I told him miserably, "but I just seem to have come to a dead end. Can you help me?"

"I don't know," he said slowly. He made a tent of his fingers, and gazed at me thoughtfully for a long while. Then, abruptly, he asked, "Where were you happiest as a child?"

"As a child?" I echoed. "Why, at the beach, I suppose. We had a summer cottage there. We all loved it."

He looked out the window and watched the October leaves sifting down. "Are you capable of following instructions for a single day?"

"I think so," I said, ready to try anything.

"All right. Here's what I want you to do."

He told me to drive to the beach alone the following morning arriving not later than nine o'clock. I could take some lunch, but I was not to read, write, listen to the radio or talk to anyone. "In addition," he said, "I'll give you a prescription to be taken every three hours."

He tore off four prescription blanks, wrote a few words on

* Reprinted with permission of *The Reader's Digest* and Arthur Gordon.

each, folded them, numbered them, and handed them to me. "Take these at nine, twelve, three and six."

"Are you serious?" I asked.

He gave a short bark of a laugh. "You won't think I'm joking when you get my bill!"

The next morning, with little faith, I drove to the beach. It was lonely, all right. A northeaster was blowing; the sea looked gray and angry. I sat in the car, the whole day stretching emptily before me. Then I took out the first of the folded slips of paper. On it was written: *Listen carefully.*

I stared at the two words. Why, I thought, the man must be mad. He had ruled out music and newscasts and human conversation. What else was there?

I raised my head and did listen. There were no sounds but the steady roar of the sea, the creaking cry of a gull, the drone of some aircraft high overhead. All these sounds were familiar.

I got out of the car. A gust of wind slammed the door with a sudden clap of sound. Am I supposed, I asked myself, to listen carefully to things like that?

I climbed a dune and looked out over the deserted beach. Here the sea bellowed so loudly that all other sounds were lost. And yet, I thought suddenly, there must be sounds beneath sounds—the soft rasp of drifting sand, the tiny wind-whisperings in the dune grasses—if the listener got close enough to hear them.

On an impulse I ducked down and, feeling faintly ridiculous, thrust my head into a clump of seaweed. Here I made a discovery: If you listen intently, there is a fractional moment in which everything seems to pause, wait. In that instant of stillness, the racing thoughts halt. For a moment, when you truly listen for something outside yourself, you have to silence the clamorous voices within. The mind rests.

I went back to the car and slid behind the wheel. *Listen carefully.* As I listened again to the deep growl of the sea, I found myself thinking about the immensity of it, the stupendous rhythms of it, the velvet trap it makes for moonlight, the white-fanged fury of its storms.

I thought of the lessons it had taught us as children. A certain amount of patience: You can't hurry the tides. A great deal of respect: The sea does not suffer fools gladly. An awareness of the vast and mysterious interdependence of things: Wind and tide and current, calm and squall and hurricane, all combining to determine the paths of the birds above and the fish below. And the cleanness of it all, with every beach swept twice a day by the great broom of the sea.

Sitting there, I realized I was thinking of things bigger than myself—and there was relief in that.

Even so, the morning passed slowly. The habit of hurling myself at a problem was so strong that I felt lost without it. Once, when I was wistfully eying the car radio, a phrase from Carlyle jumped into my head: "Silence is the element in which great things fashion themselves . . ."

By noon the wind had polished the clouds out of the sky, and the sea had a hard, merry sparkle. I unfolded the second "prescription." And again I sat there, half amused and half exasperated. Three words this time: *Try reaching back.*

Back to what? To the past, obviously. But why, when all my worries concerned the present or the future?

I left the car and started tramping reflectively along the dunes. The doctor had sent me on the beach because it was a place of happy memories. Maybe that was what I was supposed to reach for: The wealth of happiness that lay half-forgotten behind me.

I found a sheltered place and lay down on the sun-warmed sand. When I tried to peer into the well of the past, the recollections that came to the surface were happy but not very clear; the faces were faint and faraway, as if I had not thought of them in a long time.

I decided to experiment: To work on these vague impressions as a painter would, retouching the colors, strengthening the outlines. I would choose specific incidents and recapture as many details as possible. I would visualize people complete with dress and gestures. I would listen (carefully) for the exact sound of their voices, the echo of their laughter.

The tide was going out now, but there was still thunder in the surf. So I chose to go back 20 years to the last fishing trip I made with my younger brother. (He died in the Pacific during World War II and was buried in the Philippines.) I found now that if I closed my eyes and really tried I could see him with amazing vividness, even the humor and eagerness in his eyes that far-off morning.

In fact, I could see it all: The ivory scimitar of the beach where we were fishing, the eastern sky smeared with sunrise, the great rollers creaming in, stately and slow. I could feel the backwash swirl warm around my knees, see the sudden arc of my brother's rod as he struck a fish, hear his exultant yell. Piece by piece I rebuilt it, clear and unchanged under the transparent varnish of time. Then it was gone.

I sat up slowly. *Try reaching back.* Happy people were usually assured, confident people. If, then, you deliberately reached back and touched happiness, might there not be released little flashes of power, tiny sources of strength?

This second period of the day went more quickly. As the sun began its long slant down the sky, my mind ranged eagerly through the past, reliving some episodes, uncovering others that had been completely forgotten. For example, when I was around 13 and my brother 10, Father had promised to take us to the circus. But at lunch there was a phone call: Some urgent business required his attention downtown. We braced ourselves for disappointment. Then we heard him say, "No, I won't be down. It'll have to wait."

When he came back to the table, Mother smiled. "The circus keeps coming back, you know."

"I know," said Father. "But childhood doesn't."

Across the years I remembered this, and knew from the sudden glow of warmth that no kindness is ever really wasted, or ever completely lost.

By three o'clock the tide was out; the sound of the waves was only a rhythmic whisper, like giant breathing. I stayed in my sandy nest, feeling relaxed and content—and a little complacent. The doctor's prescriptions, I thought, were easy to take.

But I was not prepared for the next one. This time the three words were not a gentle suggestion. They sounded more like a command. *Re-examine your motives.*

My first reaction was purely defensive. There's nothing wrong with my motives, I said to myself. I want to be successful—who doesn't? I want a certain amount of recognition—but so does everybody. I want more security than I've got—and why not?

Maybe, but a small voice somewhere inside my head said, those motives aren't good enough. Maybe that's the reason the wheels have stopped going round.

I picked up a handful of sand and let it stream between my fingers. In the past, whenever my work went well, there had always been something spontaneous about it, something uncontrived, something free. Lately it had been calculated, competent—and dead. Why? Because I had been looking past the job itself to the rewards I hoped it would bring. The work had ceased to be an end in itself; it had been merely a means to make money, pay bills. The sense of *giving* something, of helping people, of making a contribution, had been lost in a frantic clutch at security.

In a flash of certainty, I saw that if one's motives are wrong, nothing can be right. It makes no difference whether you are a mailman, a hairdresser, an insurance salesman, a housewife—

whatever. As long as you feel you are serving others, you do the job well. When you are concerned only with helping yourself you do it less well. This is a law as inexorable as gravity.

For a long time I sat there. Far out on the bar I heard the murmur of the surf change to a hollow roar as the tide turned. Behind me the spears of light were almost horizontal. My time at the beach had almost run out, and I felt a grudging admiration for the doctor and the "prescriptions" he had so casually and cunningly devised. I saw, now, that in them was therapeutic progression that might well be of value to anyone facing any difficulty.

Listen carefully: To calm the frantic mind, slow it down, shift the focus from inner problems to outer things.

Try reaching back: Since the human mind can hold but one idea at a time, you blot out present worry when you touch the happiness of the past.

Re-examine your motives: This was the hard core of the "treatment," this challenge to reappraise, to bring one's motives into alignment with one's capabilities and conscience. But the mind must be clear and receptive to do this—hence the six hours of quiet that went before.

The western sky was a blaze of crimson as I took out the last slip of paper. Six words this time. I walked slowly out on the beach. A few yards below high-water mark I stopped and read the words again: *Write your worries on the sand.*

I let the paper blow away, reached down and picked up a fragment of shell. Kneeling there under the vault of the sky, I wrote several words on the sand, one above the other.

Then I walked away, and I did not look back. I had written my troubles on the sand. And the tide was coming in.

Comment

What, then, is the guiding principle?

Make your article so intriguing that the reader, once he

has begun it, will feel compelled to read every single word of it—so helpful he will feel that he has written his troubles on the sand and the tide is coming in.

REWARDS

And what of the rewards? At first you will note them in more regular sales to the small magazines. One editor will occasionally comment that he likes an article especially well, another may say your work is of professional quality. You will begin to get appreciative letters from readers. Soon you will become aware of an increase in rates from your established markets. Now and then a secondary publication will buy one of your articles. Even the big popular magazines will offer to read an article "on speculation."

You are now a full-fledged professional writer. You understand with crystal clearness why an article is worth publishing. You know that it must, in some way, help a definite group of readers and the more help it provides, the greater its value. Because of this knowledge, you are devoting your entire time to the big things of life.

Suddenly you realize how far you have come in the profession—and how terribly far you have yet to go! This gives you pause. You sense that you are standing on the brink of something of tremendous importance.

For a moment you think of certain other writers—men and women who have bridged the gap from magazines to books. You remember books which have made history: Fulton Oursler's *The Greatest Story Ever Told,* Norman Vincent Peale's *The Power of Positive Thinking* and *Stay Alive All Your Life,* J. Edgar Hoover's *Masters of Deceit,* and Catherine Marshall's *To Live Again.*

Oursler, you know, was a devout Bible student. He put

into layman's language the story which he had spent years in learning intimately—the story of a man who has done more to improve world conditions than all the armed might of the ages—Jesus Christ.

You recall that Peale, in his years as a student, minister, and humanitarian, acquired information which particularly qualified him to write on *The Power of Positive Thinking* and *Stay Alive All Your Life*. Peale had a fabulous amount of valid information on these subjects.

Now you think of J. Edgar Hoover and a pattern begins to form in your mind. He, you know, has devoted his entire life and energy to preserving and protecting America. In *Masters of Deceit* he tried to warn Americans of a danger which he knows, perhaps better than any other American.

Now your mind turns to significant facts about Catherine Marshall. While still a young woman, she lost her beloved husband Peter Marshall, the famous preacher. Although she felt this loss so keenly that she almost seemed to die, she resolved to use her remaining years as best she could. In short, she resolved to live again. Out of this terrific experience and courageous resolve came *To Live Again,* one of the most successful non-fiction books of recent times.

"When I was eleven," you recall Catherine Marshall has said, "I discovered for myself that giving is actually more fun than receiving, provided one gives himself with his gift . . ."

Giving. Each of the foregoing authors—Oursler, Peale, Hoover, and Marshall—actually gave much to the world. Through personal experience fortified by careful research each of these authors found a way to perform a major service for humanity at large—to give them something significant.

You think of these books. There is nothing phony in any of them. Each one is packed with sound help for everyone in his daily living. And each has sold millions of copies.

One significant fact—one word—clings in your mind. *Help.* That is what readers want—real help in their personal problems of living.

You look into the secret compartments of your own life for material which would be of genuine help to others. You want something that is intensely helpful to millions —something that might help a reader to become a more successful parent, more adept in dealing with the public, happier in his marital life.

And a light flashes on in your brain. You see that an experience you have had, a course of action which you followed, a bit of help which someone gave you is of terrific importance. This information in the hands of millions of people could result in a monumental amount of good.

You realize a dramatic fact: You have given birth to an idea which with proper handling can produce a best seller!

This, then, is how you can succeed as a writer. Simply heed this blueprint, this well-marked road map. It has led thousands of others to what has been called the best job on earth—writing for publication. It can do the same for you.

To a considerable degree your success in this fascinating profession depends upon how well you understand that your major function as a writer is to help a particular group of people.

You should see that every article you write gives the reader genuine help. This is the magic ingredient of which hundreds of writers have fashioned best sellers. See that you use it well!